Education and Language in the Philippines

Education and Language in the Philippines

Lorraine Pe Symaco and
Francisco P. Dumanig

LEXINGTON BOOKS
Lanham • Boulder • New York • London

Published by Lexington Books

An imprint of The Rowman & Littlefield Publishing Group, Inc.
4501 Forbes Boulevard, Suite 200, Lanham, Maryland 20706
www.rowman.com
86-90 Paul Street, London EC2A 4NE

Copyright © 2022 The Rowman & Littlefield Publishing Group, Inc.

All rights reserved. No part of this book may be reproduced in any form or by any electronic or mechanical means, including information storage and retrieval systems, without written permission from the publisher, except by a reviewer who may quote passages in a review.

British Library Cataloguing in Publication Information Available

Library of Congress Cataloging-in-Publication Data

978-1-7936-0295-4 (cloth)
978-1-7936-0297-8 (paperback)
978-1-7936-0296-1 (electronic)

Contents

Chapter 1: Introduction and Contextual Background — 1

Chapter 2: Education, Language, and Development — 15

Chapter 3: Language and National Identity — 31

Chapter 4: Language-in-Education Policies in the Philippines — 45

Chapter 5: Education, Language Policy, and Use in the Philippines — 59

Chapter 6: Education and Language: A Multi-ethnic Approach — 73

Chapter 7: Closing Remarks: Education and Language in the Philippines — 85

References — 99

Index — 123

About the Authors — 129

Chapter 1

Introduction and Contextual Background

COUNTRY CONTEXT

The Republic of the Philippines, an archipelagic country located in South East Asia, consists of more than 7,100 islands with the three main geographical locations/islands of Luzon, Visayas, and Mindanao. The diverse geographical features of the country, with a coastline of some 36,000 km, makes it one of the longest coastlines in the world, also home to varied mountainous parts and narrow coastal plains (Cullinane, 2020). The Philippines is classified as a lower-middle-income country with a per capita income (GNI) of 1,046 US Dollars, home to 106.7 million people, and a young median age of 25.7 (PSA, n.d.). It is predominantly a Christian nation, ranking 3rd globally in terms of the highest Catholic population (World Population Review, n.d.). The capital Manila is the world's most densely populated city exhibiting massive urban migration, while the Bangsamoro Autonomous Region in Muslim Mindanao (BARMM) in the southern Philippines serves as the only Muslim majority autonomous region in the country. Cultural diversity is also inherent in the Philippines, home to over 14–17 million Indigenous Peoples (IPs) belonging to 110 ethnolinguistic groups (UNDP, 2013). There are 130 recognized indigenous languages scattered across the country (KWF, n.d.), though varying accounts of actual living languages are recorded (Dayag, 2012). The official language is Filipino, while English remains the working language. Language issues remain at the forefront of educational policies, as will be discussed later, this also being linked to greater internationalization and globalization of services. As a founding member of the Association of South East Asian Nations, the World Trade Organisation, and the United Nations, the Philippines continues to prioritize international collaborations in all facets of its development.

Situated in the Pacific Ring of Fire, the country displays frequent volcanic and seismic activities, while its location in the Pacific also makes it prone to initial typhoon impacts that sustain devastating consequences to basic social services such as education (Symaco, 2013). Such geographic features make the Philippines one of the most disaster-prone countries in the world, ranked as third in the World Risk report of 2018. These characteristics also make it challenging to reach far-flung areas of the country where it is not uncommon to have areas deprived of basic utilities such as electricity. It also remains a contest for the Philippines to address the long-term socioeconomic impacts and effects of disasters, given the population's lack of disaster mitigation training despite its vulnerability to such. The role of poverty also highlights social issues that impact essential social services through the proliferation of urban poverty and socioreligious conflict in Mindanao, among others, all of which put a strain on health and education services. For instance, the destruction of schools due to the conflict in the country's south or the use of schools for evacuation purposes contributes to the disruption of education services (Symaco, 2013). With a significant percentage of the population (16.6 percent) living below the national poverty line (ADB, 2020), providing a more efficient social services model remains a challenge.

Mobility in labor employment significantly contributes to the country's economy, with a remittance of over 30 billion USD in 2019 alone from the Overseas Filipino Workers (OFWs). A leading labor exporter, the country officially deployed more than 2 million OFWs in 2016, an increase of 14.53 percent from the previous year (POEA, n.d.). This does not include the substantial number of illegal migrants who continue to look for jobs overseas with the promise of better pay than what can be offered at home. Similarly, this exodus of labor puts a strain on the country's social services, where medical professionals and teachers consist of a sizable number of those going overseas to work, with some even acceding to lower-skilled jobs. Transitioning from an agricultural-based to services and manufacturing economy, the country's information technology-business process outsourcing (IT-BPO) continues to be one of the primary job providers to its population and a noteworthy contributor to growth and development. English proficiency and a cheaper labor market both contribute to the growth of IT-BPOs in the country.

The following sections will give an overview of the country's education system and relevant language policies affecting the sector.

EDUCATION DEVELOPMENT IN THE PHILIPPINES

Beginnings and Development of Formal Education

The development of education in the Philippines before Spanish colonization in the sixteenth century was informal and focussed mainly on equipping children with vocational skills over the more formal 3Rs (reading, writing, and arithmetic). Tribal tutors who imparted education during this time were then replaced by Spanish missionaries during the Spanish colonial period, with education taking a more religious-oriented approach (DepEd, n.d.).

The Educational Decree of 1863, during the Spanish colonial period, saw the supposed expansion of access to education which required the formation of at least one primary school under each municipality. During the same time, the role of religion in education was further heightened by establishing schools for male teachers under Jesuit supervision. The influence of Spain was also reinforced by the compulsory teaching of the Spanish language, though education during this period was elitist and confined to a small percentage of the population (see Alzona, 1932). Despite the supposed improvement of access in education during this stage, the sector was then considered "inadequate, suppressed and controlled" (DepEd, n.d.).

The Spanish defeat by the Americans in 1898 eventually paved the way for the revolutionary government under the then President Emilio Aguinaldo (1899), also considered the First Philippine Republic. The provision of free and compulsory primary education was one of the main provisions of the Constitution of the newly formed government. It was also around this time during the American colonial period that the First Philippine Commission, also known as the Schurman Commission, advocated for a system of public education in the country.

Further efforts to increase development and access in education were detailed under the Second Philippine Commission (Taft Commission) through the drafting of the Education Act of 1901 and the enactment of Act 74, which established the Department of Public Instruction. The Department promoted free and accessible public instruction to all Filipinos. During this phase (1901–1902), the United States (US) government sent close to a thousand teachers to the Philippines---the first large group to arrive, of which were the Thomasites. The focus on education access during this period significantly changed the education landscape of the country. Ten years after the arrival of the Thomasites, 4,000 schools were constructed, and by the year 1920, primary level enrolment more than doubled while secondary level enrolments increased by close to 14,000 (Calata, 2002). Along with special educational institutes, the secondary education system was further established by the Philippines Commission in 1902 (DepEd, n.d.).

The Japanese occupation in the country between 1942 and 1945 also instigated some developments in the education system, where the Japanese command established the Ministry of Education in 1943. Under the Japanese administration, the "love for work and dignity for labor" was emphasized in the education system, along with the teaching of the Philippine history, the Filipino language, among others, reserved strictly for the Filipinos (DepEd, n.d.).

The Education Act of 1972 created the Ministry of Education, Culture and Sports, which was then converted to the Department of Education, Culture and Sports (DECS) in 1987, which overlooks the formal and non-formal sectors at all levels. Eventually, the Commission on Higher Education (CHED) creation in 1994 and the Technical Education and Skills Development Authority (TESDA) in 1995 has shaped the tri-focalization of education in the Philippines. The CHED oversees the higher education sector, and the TESDA governs post-secondary training and skills development. DECS was eventually renamed as the Department of Education (DepEd) in 2001 through the Governance of Basic Education Act, which also redefined the role of field offices within the department. This structure remains up to this day.

Aims and Objectives of Education

Education in the Philippines is a basic right enshrined in the Philippine Constitution, which sets out that the State "shall protect and promote the right of all citizens to quality education at all levels and shall take appropriate steps to make such education accessible to all (Philippines, 1987, Article XIV, Section 1). The Constitution also ensures the need to make education accessible by providing free primary and secondary education in public schools. It also mandates primary education to be compulsory to all Filipinos, though issues such as poverty fail to make this a reality for some (Symaco, 2013a). The significance of education for Filipinos is evident. Education is seen as a vehicle out of poverty wherein a school/university certificate would better one's chances of securing employment in an otherwise competitive labor sector.

The importance of education is also observed through the tri-focalization of educational services, aiming to serve better the different education sectors at all levels. This reorganization due to the Congressional Commission on Education (EDCOM) report in 1991 has resulted in the DepEd, CHED, and TESDA taking on specific functions to improve and manage the formal and informal education sectors.

The Governance of Basic Education (GBE) Act of 2001 provides the mandate of the Department of Education, which is to "formulate, implement, and coordinate policies, plan, programs and projects in the areas of formal and non-formal basic education" (DepEd, n.d.a). The DepEd covers levels of education until the secondary level within the public and private sector. Alternative learning systems to further ensure greater access to education are also under the influence of the Department. Aside from providing the framework for the governance of basic education in the country, the GBE Act of 2001 confirms that field offices within the Department "implement educational programs, projects and services in the communities they serve" and positions the schools and learning centers as the focal points where "schoolchildren are able to learn a range of core competencies prescribed for elementary and high school education programs or where the out-of-school youth and adult learners are provided alternative learning programs and receive accreditation for at least the equivalent of a high school education" (RA 9155, 2001, pp. 2–3). Additionally, the Enhanced Basic Education Act of 2013 also pursues the significance of education by guaranteeing that the State shall "create a functional basic education system that will develop productive and responsible citizens equipped with the essential competencies, skills and values for both life-long learning and employment" (RA 10533, 2013, p. 1).

On the one hand, the higher education sector also contributes significantly to the development policies of the Philippines. Like the DepEd, the CHED envisions the essential role of education for the country's broader development. The Higher Education Act of 1994 details the mandate of the CHED, which include among others: (a) to promote relevant and quality higher education; (b) to ensure that quality higher education is accessible to all; and (c) to guarantee and protect academic freedom for continuing intellectual growth (CHED, n.d.). Likewise, post-secondary and middle-level training within the TESDA provides substantial support to the education sector through its active involvement in technical development and skills training. As one of the principal partners of the Filipino workforce, TESDA aims to provide "direction, policies, programs, and standards toward quality technical education and skill development" (TESDA, n.d.). The agency, mandated by then the Technical Education and Skills Development Act of 1994, combines the functions of the National Manpower and Youth Council (NMYC); the Bureau of Technical-Vocational Education of the Department of Education, Culture and Sports (BTVE-DECS); and the Office of Apprenticeship of the Department of Labor and Employment (DOLE) into one office (TESDA, n.d.).

LANGUAGE POLICY AND PRACTICE IN THE PHILIPPINES

Language Policy and Use in Philippine Constitutions

The Philippines has had five Constitutions since the independence in 1896. The Malolos Constitution of 1899 required no mandate or regulation of using the languages spoken in the country, except by "virtue of law and only for acts of public authority and judicial affairs." It pointed further that the "Spanish language shall be temporarily used" (Article 93). On the one hand, under the Americans and the foundation of the Philippines Commonwealth, the 1935 Constitution then instituted the steps to adopt one of the languages in the country as a national language, while English and Spanish are to be used as official languages meantime (Article XIII, Section 3). The Institute of National Language (INL) then suggested that Tagalog be the country's national language through extensive study and consultation. This recommendation ultimately resulted in Executive Order 134 of 1937, which pronounced it as the national language of the Philippines. But given contentions over the choice of Tagalog as the national language, the term was then coined to "Pilipino" to appease the dispute.

The Japanese occupation that then followed saw the creation of the 1943 Constitution, which limited Western influence by mandating that "(t)he government shall take steps toward the development and propagation of Tagalog as the national language" (Article IX, Section 2). The short-lived 1943 Constitution was soon replaced by the reinstated 1935 Constitution when the Allied Forces liberated the country (Tan, 2014). Consequently, the 1973 Constitution under then-President Ferdinand Marcos has advanced the use of Filipino as the national language wherein the government shall "take steps towards the development and formal adoption of a common national language to be known as Filipino" and "until otherwise provided by law, English and Pilipino shall be the official languages" (Article XV, Sections 2 and 3). As will be discussed later, under Marcos' rule, bilingualism was promoted in schools by the National Board of Education (NBE). The Philippines' current Constitution (1987), formed after the collapse of the Marcos government, also reinstates Filipino as the national language and likewise promotes a bilingual language policy. And most recently, the Department of Education (in 2009) announced the mother-tongue-based multilingual education (MTB-MLE) framework in the education sector.

The MTB-MLE, Bilingual Policy and Language Preference in the Philippines

In the country's context, the MTB-MLE program is delivered as a subject area and medium of instruction (MOI). Under this scheme, fluency in the mother tongue (MT) starts at grades 1 to 3 (ages 7 to 9 years old). The MT is also used as the MOI from pre-primary to grade 3 except for subjects in Filipino (L2) and English (L3). Oral fluency, reading, and writing for L2 and L3 are to be introduced from grade 1 (DepEd Order 16, 2012). Supported by empirical findings recognized by the government from both the Lingua Franca and Lubuagan First Language projects, the MTB-MLE gains precedence through the purported academic competencies more efficiently gained by learners if taught in their first language (L1) as compared to their second or third languages (L2 and L3). Much attention is given to the MTB-MLE initiative that a university, in compliance with the 2009 institutionalization of the agenda, has offered an education graduate program specializing in MTB-MLE (DepEd Advisory 398, 2012).

Before the MTB-MLE, the Philippines had adopted a bilingual policy on education. Prompted by the National Board of Education's (NBE) inclination to promote bilingualism in schools, the then Department of Education Culture and Sports (DECS) instituted the policy on bilingual education in 1974. Bilingualism defined as the operational use of both English and Filipino as MOIs in subject areas in schools (Espiritu, 2015). The change in government and constitutional amendments followed in 1987 also emphasized using bilingual language policy, following the 1973 NBE initiative. The DECS 1987 Policy on Bilingual Education stresses the use of both Filipino and English as language subjects in all levels to achieve bilingual competence and has also promoted the use of regional languages as auxiliary languages to be taught in grades 1 and 2 (DECS order 52, 1987). Quite clearly, despite the bilingual language policy outlined in the 1987 Constitution, which emphasizes the use "(f)or purposes of communication and instruction, the official languages of the Philippines are Filipino, and until otherwise provided by law, English" (article XIV, Section 7), the nationalistic ideology in language planning was explicit in the Constitution where the development of the Filipino is seen as a "linguistic symbol of national unity and identity" (DECS order 52, 1987, p. 2).

The role of Filipino was highly accorded its due from the 1987 Constitution with the formation of the *Komisyon sa Wikang Filipino* (Commission on the Filipino Language) in 1991, which was assigned to ensure the evolution and enrichment of the Filipino language. Composed of ethnolinguists and other professionals, the Commission sought to conduct research to improve, expand, and preserve the language (KWF, 2015). The use of Filipino has further imposed its stature with Executive Order (EO) 335 issued by then-President Corazon Aquino in 1998, which required its use in all government agencies' official communications, correspondence, and transactions. The EO also required names of offices, buildings, public offices, and others to be translated into Filipino. The nationalistic tendencies are much apparent in this order which also decreed the Institute of Philippine Languages to administer an information campaign to emphasize the "importance and necessity of Filipino as an effective instrument for national unity and progress" (p. 2). Nonetheless, this move has not been without criticism, as seen by players in the private sector (Symaco, 2011).

EDUCATION AND LANGUAGE ISSUES

In this book, we shall discuss language policies and issues relevant to the education system in the Philippines. Topics related to the roles of language to development, globalization, national identity, and other cultural manifestations are examined. The order of the book is as follows: Chapters 2 and 3 present a theoretical and conceptual background to language, development, and sociocultural contexts; the role of language in national identity, among others. In Chapter 2, we review literature on development as it relates to education and language in the Philippines. Related theories that influence, broadly, education language policy formations are examined while attendant effects (e.g., ASEAN regionalization) are also discussed. Chapter 3 deals with the roles of education and language in identity formations, contextualizing such issues related to the following chapter (4). Matters that relate to language-in-education policies such as the MTB-MLE-and how this furthers the dynamics of identity formation in the county are examined. To give a more nuanced overview of related language-in-education policies in the Philippines, Chapter 4 looks at significant policies from 1974's Bilingual Education to the more recent MTB-MLE of 2009. Significant educational reforms that interplay with these policies are also reviewed.

For Chapters 5 and 6, more thematic approaches to education and language issues are identified. The role of globalization in education, in particular, the use of the English language for "modernity," is discussed in Chapter 5. The significant part of English in education and broader development as it relates to policies and actual language use and practice, is also taken into account. The multi-ethnic and linguistic features of the Philippines are re-assessed in Chapter 6 alongside issues of inclusion, identity-formation, and marginalized languages. The particular role of the MTB-MLE policy, which tries to address such concerns---and the inherent complications faced by this policy regarding teacher training, resources, and non-use of policy in specific settings are also deliberated. Lastly, Chapter 7 integrates the different issues raised in the book, contextualizing these within the frameworks discussed in Chapters 2 and 3. The way forward in terms of education policy formation for advancement is considered, also acknowledging issues in education and language as relevant to the Philippines.

The following sections will discuss the themes of education, language, and development; and the sociocultural political manifestations of language as explored in subsequent chapters.

Education, Language, and Development

Throughout this book, the role of education and language in development is highlighted, considering the varied frameworks of development from earlier accounts of the human capital approach, modernization, and dependency theories---to the more recent New Growth Theory as it applies to greater regionalization and intensified role of the knowledge-economy. We see the investments in human capital training espoused by the move toward greater globalization of services, pushing the commodification of education as mobility across borders denote the ever-changing landscape of the education sector. Along with this stems the need for greater standardizations---defined through benchmarking of qualifications and the rise of high-stakes international assessments. This has also brought forward the appeal for a standard and global language. The influence of the English language surfaces toward this broader move to development, from the preferred language used in employment, training institutions, and governments. Variations of development theories accounting for the post-modernist approach, which takes into consideration economic and sociopolitical hegemony is noted where New Growth Theory empirics, for instance, capitalize on the more significant role of knowledge-spaces for a region's or country's progress. Such endogenous growth theories utilize technologies and human capital formation as a source of socioeconomic advancement. But while such growth theories somehow diminish the sociocultural factors or reductionist bias in earlier development frameworks, the issue of center versus periphery is still ever-present, where the lack of technological services or other related resources might disadvantage one region or location over the other.

With earlier parts of the book setting the tone on these development frameworks, we link the role of language in basic social services (education as defined here) and the function of language-in-education policies in development. We explore how formal institutions such as schools or universities, through language, might benefit a particular group over another, as exemplified, for instance, through the media of instruction in educational institutions, competitive international assessments, or employment opportunities.

The rise of English as the language of modernity gains ground from these development approaches, further heightened by the increase in internationalization and greater regionalization. The case of the 10-member countries Association of Southeast Asian Nations (ASEAN) formation is taken as an example that highlights the growing influence of the English language---from being adopted as the organization's working language to the need to equip proficiency among its country members in line with education and employment-related mobilities across the region.

Given the focus on education and language in development, it is crucial to contextualize relevant language-in-education policies in the Philippines. While this book focuses more on policies stemming from 1974's Bilingual Education Policy and the more recent MTB-MLE in 2009, various procedures have also been instituted. For instance, the Philippine Commission Act 74 in 1901, when then US President William McKinley institutionalized the public education system of the Philippines using English as a MOI. The adoption of Tagalog as the national language (eventually romanticized to Filipino in the following years) followed in 1937 through Executive Order 134 but highlighting still that "such an adoption of the Philippine National Language shall not be understood as in any way affecting the requirement that the instruction in the public schools shall be primarily conducted in the English language." The national language was then required to be taught in all public and private schools around the country in 1940, alongside the printing of the Tagalog-English dictionary (Executive Order 263).

Additionally, the National Board of Education introduced in 1957 a multilingual approach where the local vernacular was the MOI in grades 1 and 2, with Tagalog being taught informally from grade 1 and emphasized in higher grade levels. English was to be taught as a subject from earlier grade levels and transitioned as MOI from grade 3. However, such an approach was heavily criticized due to "the observed weakness of the multilingual policy which it promoted. The use of no less than four languages (English, Pilipino, Spanish, and the vernacular) did not prove effective in educating the Filipino child" (Clemente, n.d.). Because of the multilinguistic features of the Philippines, concerns regarding the choice of language in education are extant. Inextricably linked here are the sociocultural manifestations of language and often the perceived biases concerning one's language priming. Such issues figure closely in our discussions, investigating such roles in language-in-education policies in the Philippines. We shall examine briefly in the next section such matters as relevant to our country context.

Sociocultural and Political Manifestations of Language

The multi-ethnic and linguistics features of the Philippines highlight all the more the related cultural and political underpinnings of language pursued in literature (Chomsky, 2004; Kramsch, 1998). In the following chapters, we see the dynamics of education and language at play in the Philippines related to progress goals and individual mobility advancements so desired by its population. The political nuances of language choice are mirrored from the most central—the choice of the national language Filipino, despite some opposing views to this preference. It is argued that political hegemony stems from the selection of Filipino as the national language (romanticized from Tagalog and Pilipino), being the vernacular of the country's center of political power (i.e., Manila). As discussed in the previous section, we have seen how language policies in education have shifted from the Bilingual Education Policy stemming from the desire to "balance the legitimate aspirations of nationalism . . . and an equally legitimate desire to maintain English as a Language of Wider Communication" (Gonzales 1990, p. 153).

This view of English as an imminent medium for greater access to the sciences and other opportunities was in motion decades before the more celebrated notions of globalization or commodification of education now. The difference now is we see a more pervasive form of English domination as it links to high-stakes assessments and better job prospects, among other things. While the world continues to get more interconnected due to technological advancements, the issue of access is ever-present where the "appropriate" socioeconomic background might enable one to maximize the use of resources in such a context. On the one hand, the long-promoted idea of cultural capital, which inherently perpetuates the command of established social structures that links to grounding to the right background (family ties, educational access), is marked. Coalescing the two premises, Bourdieu's cultural capital is argued to point to, "knowledge of or facility with 'highbrow' aesthetic culture [and] . . . cultural capital is analytically and causally distinct from other essential forms of knowledge or competence (technical skills, human capital, etc.) (Lareau and Weininger 2003, p. 567). The apparent association to this concept and studies of inequality brings forth some of the arguments in this book when language-in-education policies favor groups primed with the intrinsic language skills (i.e., Filipino) or a more proficient version of the supposed language for modernity (i.e., English).

Language policy and national identity also prefigure in our work, tying the multi-ethnic feature of the country to language policies as affecting the Filipinos. Of course, we take into account the compound definitions of identity---whether "inhabited" or "achieved"---or even the nuanced discussion of nation-states as it relates to identity formation (Blommaert 2006, p. 238), where the latter is unavoidably influenced by globalization, bringing us back full circle to the issues of development prospects as earlier defined. More intricate considerations of linguistic and speech communities by Silverstein (1998) puts into context a multilingual communicative practice, taken for example in the Philippines through the introduction of the MTB-MLE and the continued use of English, and the need to promote Filipino if only but to enable access to top-performing educational institutions in the country, mostly (but not limited to) located in Manila. Issues of rights to access as may be defined by language-in-education policies is a popular notion in related multilinguistic debates (Hornberger, 1998; Skutnabb-Kangas, 2001), as we may also have presaged, where we view the introduction of the MTB-MLE as a means to enhance better teaching and learning in schools, which then supposedly signifies improved socioeconomic mobilities.

This argument of the privileged use of language in education and culture is also seen mainly as "ideological or political, or at best, pragmatic" (Hobsbawn 1996, p. 1072), where it comes at odds in terms of mass literacy when there is disjoint in terms of language-in-education use and the spoken vernacular. However, as indivisibly linked to development concerns of the Philippines, we also consider the need to balance the socioeconomic ecologies especially relevant in poorer countries and language rights. The resources required to maintain a language might find more value in investments in other social services that are deemed lacking. Bearing in mind the influence of globalization and the need to standardize services, we take much to ponder education and language issues. While not discounting the possible abysmal loss of a language and supporting concerns of the need to save one's culture through language use, we echo Mufwene (2010, p.929) in asking: "What are a particular heritage language and a corresponding static culture good for if the relevant population feels these disadvantage them?" Despite the discussion brought forward in this book on the links of language to relevant notions (culture, capital, etc.), we do not propose to resolve the complex and nuanced dynamics of education and language. Nonetheless, we hope that by further contextualizing the dynamics of education and language in the Philippines, we can feature actualities that should be considered in every language-in-education policy pronouncement since a society is only as equipped as its weakest link.

Note

Parts of this chapter are taken from Lorraine Symaco's "Education, language policy and language use in the Philippines." *Language Problems and Language Planning*. 41(4), 2017, pp 87–102, John Benjamins, DOI: 10.1075/lplp.41.1.05sym. https://benjamins.com/catalog/lplp. and Lorraine Symaco's

"Teacher education in the Philippines." In K.G. Karras & C.C. Wolhuter (Eds.) *International Handbook on Teacher Education Worldwide*, pp261–372. Cyprus: HM Studies and Publishing, 2010. Reprinted with permission.

Chapter 2

Education, Language, and Development

INTRODUCTION

The role of education for development is highlighted in literature. In line with the increasing internationalization of services, factors influencing broader growth in countries through government policies are mirrored at global, regional, and local levels (Ball, 2012; Ertl, 2006). The rising trend of benchmarking through international assessments and the push for greater mobility and exchange in the education sector exemplifies the growing trend of cross-border provision, all in line to achieve more significant development for countries. While contextual considerations affect the alignment of education policies in nations, the rise of globalization is seen as a shared drive for advancement where equipping one's human resource with the needed skills for the knowledge economy is crucial. The following sections will discuss the role of education for development alongside attendant factors such as greater regionalism, modernity, and sociopolitical and cultural factors as affecting such.

DEVELOPMENT FRAMEWORKS

Theories for socioeconomic development exhibit varying tendencies from the role of societal engagement to modernity, Marxist to Keynesian, and ranging from long-established rationales to the more recent approaches in line with increasing regionalization and globalization of services. Fletcher some time ago defined development as "the actualization of an implicit potentiality" (1974, p. 43). This implicit potentiality defines laying the groundwork for improvement in societies where growth in any "potential" level is likened to a move toward progress. Looking at selected theories of development, we see the implied roles of education and proposed "equalization" in societies and the move toward "modernity" for advancement.

The foundations of human capital theory as espoused by Theodore Schultz in the 1960s focuses on the role of education for development where a supplement volume in 1962 in the *Journal of Political Economy* investigated the "Investment in Human Beings," while notable works such as Gary Becker's *Human Capital* sets further the groundwork for the theory (Blaug, 1976). The main argument for a country's development as relying on its human resources has validated many investments and expansions in education in line with this thought. For policymakers, economic development continues to be of national importance, where human capital theory is akin to growth if human capital is determinedly developed. For instance, older studies point to a skilled labor force as a determining factor for growth, as exhibited in the work of Solow (1957), which attributed 90 percent of progress in the USA between 1930 and 1955 as relying on technical progress. Eventually, the push for human capital theory gained traction as countries, in their desires to advance progress, move from agriculture to manufacturing-based industries. At the same time, international declarations such as the Education for All (EFA) further strengthens this idea. The rise of globalization and the push for greater internationalization of standards and services continues to demonstrate the influence of the human capital approach in global government policies. Despite this, critiques of the theory describe this as a "one-dimensional normative framework" (see Bowles and Gintis, 1975) that fails to take into account how human capital development further exacerbate inequities in societies and, where success in further studies and training is primarily predisposed to socioeconomic backgrounds as cultivated by such inequalities in the first place.

The new comparative politics in the 1950s has exhibited an increased focus on the non-western, "developing" world to understand its development better while embracing this theory of modernization. The idea of "modernization" dominant in post-war development studies has given rise to the blanket traditional versus modern society as espoused by the modernization theory wherein development is equated through the achievement of the "modern society" largely determined by Western ideals. This ethnocentric bias runs clear in Macaulay's idea of forming an Indian Civil Service with "a class of persons Indian in blood and colour, but English in tastes, in opinion, in morals and in intellect" (see Bernstein 1971, p. 147). Such Western ideological considerations remain one of the main criticisms of this approach, while defenders propose that such ideological purpose serves to benefit more than weaken national institutions. Variations have since developed from post-modernism to neoliberalism in line with economic and sociopolitical hegemony. Despite this, a lack of plurality and a reductionist bias from these development theories is argued, where geographical and sociohistorical diversity is often not recognized within these frameworks (Brohman, 1995).

Structural inequalities within countries and societies also make it challenging to attain an idealized framework for development. Arguing for a more relativist approach in development theories, we note the significance of contextualization in understanding development processes in countries, taking into account the local context and other sociocultural dynamics (e.g., language, ethnicity) in play that is often disregarded in neoclassical economic frameworks. The universal applicability of economic growth in these arguments accounts for development as "neither culture-specific nor is it based on historically changing conditions" where "variations in historical or sociocultural circumstances are treated as 'noise' that should be filtered out to increase the parsimony of development models" (ibid, p. 123). Frameworks that aim to address structural inequalities as undermined by other models (e.g., dependency theory and Wallerstein's neo-Marxist world systems theory) construct the core-periphery approach, but with variations in terms of attaining democratization and development. Similar to neoclassical economic frameworks, such models are criticized for their over-generalization and lack of balance, where culture is ignored in the pattern for development (Christofis, 2019).

EDUCATION FOR DEVELOPMENT

The task of education for greater progress with the situation drawn above in rough exhibits the particular link of government policies around the world with varied theories of development---from training its population with the needed skills as advocated by the human capital approach to the inclination to push for modernity in sync with globalization. There is no justice in oversimplifying the role of education as it links to the theories above, given the complexities and nuances that describe the various models and the process of education itself. The role of culture often missed in neoclassical economics, and the oversimplification of the core and periphery aspects requires a more cohesive approach in likening the role of education for the development of countries. Apart from the more distinct economic indicators, sociocultural and political realities that define education policies as it links to progress is equally essential, or at the very least to be considered in terms of aligning to development goals.

The idea of human capital for economic development is not new. Adam Smith mentions the need to accumulate private, social, and human capital, alongside the role of technologies for progress (Goldsmith, 1995). The field of *economics of education* developed in the 1950s pertains to the focus beyond the traditional inputs (land, labor, and other physical capital) for national development (Psacharopoulos, 1988) and where the mystery of a "residual" in predicting economic growth beyond the conventional inputs was attributed to education and human capital (Schultz, 1961; Pang and Hassan, 1976). Studies have since focused on, among others, the returns to the investment of education and labor market outcomes. In addition, international calls to focus on the rights to education similarly highlight the importance of education for development---from the EFA program in 1990 with follow up of the Dakar Framework for Action in 2000, while the Millennium Development Goals (MDGs) also included the universal primary education call. The most recent Sustainable Development Goals (SDG) 2030 also features education (as SDG4).

It is therefore not surprising to see the number of investments in the sector. For instance, despite existing disparities, primary education has seen an increase in developing nations' enrollment from 52 percent in 1990 to 78 percent in 2012 (UNDP, n.d.). In 2016, an increase in education aid was documented despite being below the identified amount needed to reach the levels for SDG4. The 2015 Addis Ababa Action Agenda was also set to discuss a global framework for financing the 2030 SDG goals, including the SGD4 for quality education (UNESCO, 2018). A worldwide expansion in higher education was also witnessed (Schofer and Meyer, 2005), where roughly 500,000 students were enrolled in higher education institutions in the year 1900, to 100 million by 2000. That "beyond the national factors affecting educational expansion that are normally discussed, global factors are involved. They impact educational growth in every part of the world, driving massive expansion" (ibid, p. 918). This trend has continued across the globe, where national governments continue to invest in higher education in line with their commitment to improve development and rise in sync with the demands of globalization (Marginson and van der Wende, 2007).

The situation above rings true in the Philippines, where investments in the education sector highlight its recognized role in development. In 2019, education took the top spot in allocation (at 18.16 percent or 665.1 Billion Philippine Pesos, Php) of the total national budget (DBM, 2019). Such investment in education is also mirrored in previous national budgets where the sector continues to favor allocations. The Philippines Development Plan likewise underlines the significance of human capital development through mobility, better education, and health. It "recognizes human development not just as a means to an end (i.e., human capital as a factor of production) but also an end in itself (NEDA 2017, p. 137) and where "diverse and dynamic working environments that come with further economic integration require twenty-first-century skills among graduates [which will] . . . develop life skills necessary to succeed in a competitive workplace (ibid, p. 146). Policies that aim to achieve a more relevant education sector were also recently introduced in the Philippines, such as the Transnational Higher Education Law in 2019, the K12 Education Programme in 2012, and the Mother Tongue-Based Multilingual Education (MTB-MLE) in 2009. The Government has also introduced programs and strategies intending to improve access to education for the most deprived through its conditional cash transfer program (CCT)---the *Pantawid Pamilyang Pilipino Program (4Ps)*, and the Universal Access to Quality Tertiary Education Act of 2017 which institutionalized free tuition fees in state universities and colleges, local universities, and colleges in the Philippines. Notwithstanding such policies meant for more significant education development and access, some said programs are mired with controversies due to the lack of proper consultations and efficiencies, alongside existing corruption within the system (Reyes, 2010; Symaco, 2011, 2017).

Globalization

The sections above show the increasing prominence of education for development as highlighted by the massification of education alongside increasing investments in the sector. Development frameworks that set the role of human capital and modernity mirror broadly call for progress, exemplified by a skilled labor force combined with its neoliberal tendencies. The rise of international assessments and the introduction of the university rankings system highpoints the market-oriented feature of education. As an illustration, highly placed universities that figure in ranking systems continue to attract a significant number of students while a more "customized" feature of this, such as ranking institutions by subject excellence, also facilitates the choice of universities by prospective students. International assessment exercises such as OECD's Programme for International Student Assessment (PISA) and the Trends in International Mathematics and Science Study (TIMSS) also figure in this tendency, where countries try to emulate success stories, and national investments in education are invested in further improving already highly-placed institutions (World Bank 2016; Sellar and Lingard 2013).

In particular, this integration of education in higher education institutions in the new economy underscores academic capitalism, where it "moves beyond the thinking of the student as consumer to considering institutions as marketers. When students choose colleges, institutions advertise education as a service and a lifestyle. Colleges and universities compete vigorously to market their institutions (Slaughter and Rhoades 2004, p.1). The commodification of education is further exemplified by the General Agreement on Trade in Services (GATS) that covers the cross-border provision of education where it is seen as a tradable commodity, further implicating its neo-liberal constitutionalism (Scherrer 2005). Notwithstanding the debate between education as a commodity or a public good (see Grace 1989), the ease and increase in mobility, alongside greater calls for regionalism, have strengthened institutional cooperation and cross-border provision of educational services, all in line with the need to capitalize on knowledge production and sharing to further development. It should also be noted that greater chances of success for both mobility prospects and assessments would also require the ability to communicate and understand a language. This argument brings us to the linked sociocultural dynamics of language to be discussed later.

The commodification of education, as aforementioned, links to the broad call for increased knowledge-based in the population, where progress is tied to a highly skilled workforce crucial in the knowledge-based society (Symaco, 2012). Empirics of regional convergence follow this line, from the propositioned New Growth Theory by Paul Romer, which features the dominant part of knowledge for growth, where the former is not subjected to diminishing returns than physical capital. Additionally, the rise of endogenous growth theories that capitalize on technologies and human capital as a source of growth or progress---also underscores the development approach of education. It gives an alternative to neoclassical growth theories that takes the exogenous approach of such factors since human capital, increasing returns and technology, as critical factors stressed in endogenous growth theory, "develop unevenly across the space economy and are locally and regionally differentiated" (Martin and Sunley 1998, p. 220). Taking such exogenous factors makes for "possible explanations of global-local interactions and the dynamics of regional growth, most of which revolve around the proposed connections among these [such] key factors" (ibid, p. 220). Despite this, it is criticized that the endogenous growth theory approach fails to "capture the importance of the socioinstitutional context and embeddedness of regional economic development" (ibid, p. 220). The concept of "institutional thickness" (Amin and Thrift 1995) similarly envisions the contribution of institutions clustered in regions and space, promoting pathways to progress. This idea promotes the advantage of forming clusters where several institutions add to development over a space with "thin" or fewer institutions that are less likely to promote advancement. Notwithstanding critics of this concept (see Raco 1998), the broad considerations of regional convergence have given way to the rise in regionalism expressed in differing dynamics.

Such an idea has also prompted greater mobility among populations, as seen in the Bologna Process, which has created the European Higher Education Area. The push for greater standardization of degrees coupled with the rise of globalization has seen a dramatic rise in movements among students and academic staff. Looking at South East Asia, a similar though much less established move for greater regionalization in education is also pushed. From the three-country alliance (Malaysia, Philippines, and Thailand) of the Association of Southeast Asia in 1961 to the founding of the Association of

South East Asian Nations (ASEAN) in 1967 (with the addition of Indonesia and Singapore) highlights similar calls for regionalization and cooperation. The ASEAN has continued to form cooperation (now with ten country members) to elevate the socioeconomic and political orientations of the region. More localized integrations and clusters are also exemplified, for example, through the anticipated rise of education regional hubs as ambitioned by the Malaysian government (Symaco and Wan, 2017), while highly ranked universities in Singapore cement their place in this competitive higher education markets area. In the Philippines, the focus on greater education provision through increased mobility and cooperation is anticipated in the aforementioned Transnational Higher Education Law with "a view to making higher education globally competitive, attracting a flow of talented students, faculty, and staff and improving the country's human resource base" (Parrocha, 2019).

The idea of clustering, as mentioned above, also gathers momentum in the formation of dedicated spaces for development, for example, the Multimedia Super Corridor (MSC) in Malaysia, which was formed in 1996 to further its digital economy and to provide both expertise and training for the needs of the knowledge economy. Universities in the MSC, such as the Multimedia University, aim to complement this push for resource development though critics of the actual innovation capabilities of the MSC do exist (Huff, 2002; Loheswar, 2019). In the Philippines, these innovation spaces are also seen in the University of the Philippines Techohub in 2006. Partnered with a private corporation for investment purposes, criticisms over the actual innovation and its furtive privatization features beset this development (Valente, 2020). Both cases draw attention to the argument of actual efficiency of institutions (over quantity) in terms of the ability to attain progress (Rodriguez-Pose, 2013), often missed in the argument of simply "expanding and clustering" institutions in line with related government development policies.

ASEAN Engagement

With the launch of the ASEAN Economic Community (AEC) in 2015, several initiatives have been set to optimize the role of education for more remarkable development and cooperation in the region. Building on the AEC Blueprint 2015, the 2025 Blueprint likewise builds on five interrelated goals for growth, namely to promote: (i) A Highly Integrated and Cohesive Economy; (ii) A Competitive, Innovative, and Dynamic ASEAN; (iii) Enhanced Connectivity and Sectoral Cooperation; (iv) A Resilient, Inclusive, People-Oriented, and People-Centred ASEAN; and (v) A Global ASEAN (ASEAN Secretariat 2015, p. 1). These objectives stress the need to provide for human resources in the region to sustain the needed development of the ASEAN. The need to optimize movements of skills contributes to this where similar to the movement of labor in regions like the EU, skilled labor within the ASEAN is made possible through mutual recognition arrangements (MRAs) among eight professions and the broader harmonization of higher education. This free movement across borders through the MRA is permitted through mutual recognition of qualifications and implementing the ASEAN Qualifications Reference Framework (AQRF) (ASEAN Secretariat, 2015). The expanse of standardization in education does not spare the region of this trend, where the attainment of such makes for a more compact and dynamic movement among its population, which further facilitates the greater exchange of know-how and services. However, the standardization of qualifications might prove to be more challenging to attain in the ASEAN given countries' more diverse socioeconomic realities. For example, a highly industrialized Singapore with a developed education system might lack a counterpart in post-conflict Cambodia. Equally, the use (and proficiency) in a common language in this multi-ethnic region is also crucial for the success of a better integrated ASEAN. As will be discussed in other chapters, the prominence of the English language for linked mobility prospects is evident.

The focus on research and development, innovations, and technology commercialization are also driven alongside ASEAN's trek for advancement. This goal rests on the productivity of the region's labor force in addition to the crucial role of universities in this regard. In promoting such intentions, it is anticipated that there should be a promotion of "strategic partnerships among the academia, research institutions and the private sector toward developing capabilities" and "information sharing and networking to stimulate ideas and creativity at the universities and business-level (ASEAN Secretariat, 2015, pp. 16–17). Several initiatives aimed at improving the education sector of the ASEAN are also set, such as, among others, the ASEAN+3 Working Plan, which includes cooperation among ASEAN member states with China, Korea, and Japan in terms of higher education involvement. The ASEAN University Network (AUN), on the one hand, also functions in terms of optimizing skills and resources sharing and cooperation among the ten ASEAN higher education institutions (HEIs) (see Symaco and Tee, 2019). The Philippines have three top-performing universities as part of the thirty members AUN. Of course, it must be noted that this network comprises a minimal representation of HEIs across the region, which may question the efficacy of such an organization in terms of providing for a better integrated higher education sector. In addition to higher education collaborations, a broader focus on education, science, and culture is set through the Southeast Asian Ministers of Education Organization (SEAMEO) formation in 1965. It currently has twenty-six specialist institutions in the region, with the SEAMEO Regional Centre for Educational Innovation and Technology (INNOTECH) located in Manila, Philippines.

The apparent focus on education in the ASEAN is evident with the numerous though sometimes inter-lapping education programs set to develop further the sector. With the tread for a greater regional integration, the role of education is considered crucial in maintaining and providing the needed human resources to achieve this goal. This trend is also observed in the Philippines, where education services for socioeconomic advancement are observed. For instance, capitalizing on the changing features and demands of the sector, the Philippines aims to improve its internationalization feature by attracting international students and improving international collaborations through the aforementioned Transnational Higher Education Law. Greater social responsibility among its HEIs is also envisioned in response to the changing dynamics of society, parallel to the call for an inclusive, resilient, and global ASEAN (Symaco and Tee, 2018). However, challenges remain, where the country's internationalization efforts are lacking compared to its richer and more developed counterparts, while a focus on academic quality assurance efforts might put into periphery the stride toward university social responsibility.

SOCIOCULTURAL DYNAMICS OF LANGUAGE

Education's function in development through improved human resources training is mirrored in related policies in the ASEAN, as discussed above. We also discussed how theories in development illustrate this human capital approach which mainly relies on education in the process. While the effects of globalization and the broader trade of education services impinge on the changing dynamics of the sector, government policy orientations across countries inevitably capitalize on their education systems to move forward their goals for advancement. The sociocultural dynamics influence in education is also acknowledged, for instance, through the use of language-in-education policies. At the same time, the desire for greater mobility requires individuals to adapt to the language requirements of their receiving countries. Such undercurrents reflect the sociocultural subtleties of language, where complex manifestations are reflected from communications, political undertows, critical self-assessment, and education policies, among others (see Symaco, 2017; Fitch and Sanders, 2004; Levinson, 2003).

The involved link to culture is acknowledged since "language is the principal means whereby we conduct our social lives. When it is used in the contexts of communication, it is bound up with culture in multiple and complex ways" (Kramsch, 1998, p. 3). As also mirrored in social services such as education, this influence of language is exhibited through the rise of mother tongue and multilingual-based education (Rosekran, Sherris, and Chatry-Komarek, 2012;

Burton, 2013), where such influence is often backed up by cultural and political realism. For instance, Malaysia's cyclic reversal of English and *Bahasa Melayu* language use in Mathematics and Sciences course is often attributed to the persuading of the population's Malay majority of their influence in government. Similarly, the political undertone of language is also reflected in the protests over the choice of Hindi over Tamil as India's national language, Pakistan's Urdu versus Bengali, Sinhala in Sri Lanka, and Arabic in Algeria (Hobsbawn, 1996). In the Philippines, the choice of Filipino as a national language is not without controversy, with Filipino complying with the phonemes of *Tagalog*, the main language used in the imperial capital of Manila (Baumgartner, 1999).

Related to this discussion is Vygotsky's sociocultural approach which contends that the human mind is influenced not only by the physical world but also by symbiotic tools and particularly language, "to mediate and regulate our relationships with others and with ourselves and thus change the nature of these relationships" (Lantolf, 2000, p. 1). It is argued that physical or symbolic tools are passed on from one generation to the next, where "each generation reworks its cultural inheritance to meet the needs of its communities and individuals" (ibid, p. 2). In the same way, that language is "reworked" and acceded to the community and plays an essential factor in its conservancy. Language endangerment, for instance, in a minority or ethnic population, signals the possible loss of culture through the absence of its primary language. Given the shift for uniformity and the rising trends of internationalization, the idea of conformity and unity through a primary language often supersedes cultural preservation. The use of a common language inspired to promote better understanding, especially when endorsed through national policies (e.g., medium of instruction in schools; official language in government correspondence), often endangers a local language and the culture that goes with it (Fishman, 1996). This pressure for both linguistic and cultural unity results in the displacement of minority cultures should their local languages be lost. Cases of such language loss also span from the move to inculcate and practice a preferred language in governance, often from groups that exercise political (and military) power (Dorian, 1998).

This argument mirrors the issue raised above over the choice of Filipino as the national language in the Philippines. The underestimated consideration of the various languages in the country also predisposes to this "imperial" national language choice. The debasing of possibly rich languages to mere dialects in the Philippines attuned the latter more to "folklore rather than creative literature in its own right (Baumgartner, 1999. p. 165). Given such concerns, the issue of language restoration (frequently also credited to better learning as implored in relevant mother-tongue language-based education) draws focus on the role of educational institutions, where the school experience is considered to maintain languages that are or might be lost in the process of cultural and linguistic unity (Hornberger, 1998a). This idea draws contention since the restoration of language through its acquisition in the school experience (over the mother tongue) is deemed problematic. It focuses mainly on literacy and relegates its cultural dimension. Since reversing language shifts "needs to include strategies directed toward family life, culture building, and promoting a sense of community" (Fishman, 1996, p. 80).

The evolution of the study of language from its structural dimensions to roles in information and communications and as it relates to the social milieu is also noted (Spolsky, 2005). With the influence of language in sociocultural and political settings, several studies have investigated the role of language in development as it relates, among others, to teaching and learning, multiculturalism, and cognitive functions (Fitch and Sanders, 2004; Levinson, 2003; Kirkpatrick, 2012). Apart from the political overtones of language choice, its span on cultural development occurs through foreign language learning, while its proposed multiculturalism effects have been observed. References to sociolinguistics also highlight this substantial impact of language as it relates to the social environment. For instance, through the evolution of the Summer Institute of Linguistics (SIL) from linguistic descriptions of unstudied languages to the SIL International, which now focuses on "sociolinguistic analyses of the use of the languages it is dealing with and of the multilingual patterns which they share" (Spolsky, 2005, p. 255).

Language Culture and Identity

So far, we have discussed the role of language in the conservancy of culture, defining the function of language in our social lives (Sapir ,1968). The common experience that people share as evident through their use of language features the point that it embodies and symbolizes cultural reality (Kramsch, 1998, p. 3). This social identification with a language stresses its cultural value since "speakers identify themselves and others through their use of language; they view their language as a symbol of their social identity. The prohibition of its use is often perceived by its speakers as a rejection of their social group" (ibid, p. 3). Expanding this view also elucidates often the political overtones where the contest of languages and identities, as earlier discussed, shows the prominence of its power in policies---from media of instruction in schools and business to identifying a national language often disputed in multi-ethnic societies.

Cultural imperialism is also underscored when colonial powers use language to subdue populations through the spread of the colonial language or, contrastingly, the prohibition of such. This acculturation process also extends to the broadening influence of globalization, where the identification of *the* language for modernity has changed the dynamics of language education and training (Symaco, 2017). Along with this is the debate of which appropriate culture to refer to concerning foreign language learning. For instance, the role of target language culture in teaching and learning in English as a Foreign Language (EFL) settings delineates the considerable role of culture in successful language use (Alptekin, 1993). This intercultural mediation in literature has also seen a shift from its onset focus on the issue of communications among different cultures (i.e., intercultural competence) to the ability to critically compare and interpret cultures, capitalizing on the sense-making process (Liddicoat, 2014).

> Language is then not a tool lying outside culture that allows cultures to be mediated, but rather the act of mediation involves an interpretation of language itself as a culturally contexted, culturally shaped phenomenon. (ibid, p. 262)

This argument bodes language well beyond its linguistic form, where a culturally grounded use of it may assist in language teaching and learning and derive the conceptual 'identity' formed from such. The position of language in the production of identity (Bucholtz and Hall, 2004) has elicited studies in linguistic anthropology, which looked at the various processes involved. Studies have concentrated on the linguistic evidence on identity construction, for instance, from narratives, interviews, media discourses—all of which acknowledge the "role of language plays in the formation of cultural subjectivities" (ibid, p. 369). The semiotic associations of language also allow for a referent in terms of how a speaker would indirectly assume an identity (see Bucholtz and Hall, 2004).

Pierre Bourdieu's habitus or cultural capital also figures the function of language in social class, though met with criticisms (see Myles, 1999), but not discounting the influence of modernity on actual language use and practice. The latter further demarcates the "haves" and "have-nots," as we shall see in the following chapters. Other studies defining the role of class in discourse analysis (Bernstein, 1962; Halliday, 1993) also illuminate the role of language in the social milieu earlier defined. This internal and dialectical relationship between language and society shows the social phenomena of language itself (Fairclough, 1989; Sapir, 1968). Relatedly within this context, the role of education--particularly language training, draws an asset from its ability to determine socioeconomic mobilities, extending the concept of social class further related to language abilities. Relatively, the influence of language policies as vehicles to instigating or fostering social classes may be seen in mandatory policies as earlier defined (e.g., media of instruction of communication in institutions).

LANGUAGE AND DEVELOPMENT

The intricate position of language in culture and identity formation, as earlier discussed, ranges from, among others, cultural and identity formation, its utilization for gaining political control, to its use for education efficiency. This social significance of language was pointed out long ago by Durkheim and Weber, while more contemporary studies reassess this relationship (Bernstein, 1971; Fairclough, 1989). The contribution of language to broader development is also highlighted in similar policy formations often linked to political motivations. For instance, the shift of media of instruction in schools, though instigated by the desire for teaching and learning efficiency, might also draw on political motivations, relying on the control and authority manifestations of languages in populations. The relation between language and power has been discussed in varying contexts but essentially upholds its commanding role in broader development. The social conditions of language related to institutional levels also make it disposed to possible struggles with the desire of one group to maintain command over another, for instance, through the contested national language selections as earlier defined.

In the Philippines, such contention is reflected in national language selection when Baumgartner (1999) reflected on " what right could the language of one ethnic group, even if that group lived in the national capital, be imposed on the others?" (p. 169). Such disputes eventually paved the way to revising the national language to "Filipino" which "is a fusion or conglomeration of different regional dialects (sic) such as Cebuano, Waray Waray, Tagalog, etc. which are spoken in the Philippines" (ibid, p. 169), but notwithstanding criticisms to this reality. The indicators of power in a language demonstrate the advantage of cultural capital where people with access to standardization---in this case, the preferred language (see Fairclough, 1989) can perpetuate the social divisions of classes already existing. Inherent to those with access to a preferred language, this benefits them, mainly when policies are rooted in their favor. Take, for instance, an education policy that would support language X as a medium of instruction. People without the existing cultural capital or know-how of such language X might find it harder to succeed in an environment dominated by this preferred language. Moreover, while education is often seen as a "great equalizer," the differential access to educational institutions further perpetuates the one-dimensional normative critique of this human capital approach.

As earlier discussed, varying socioeconomic backgrounds dictate such differential access that can further exacerbate social inequity. The theory of cultural reproduction by Bourdieu also features the existing segregating factors of education. Despite contentions from others (see Jenkins, 2002;

Goldthorpe, 2007), Bourdieu's theory has maintained a solid theoretical standpoint where various studies have looked at education's role in cultural capital and reproduction, with most highlighting the Weberian concept of elite/status cultures (Di Maggio, 1982). This impact of class over other measured ability in schools point to this possible elite status approach which capitalizes on shared conventions for cultural attributes

> bound together by personal ties and a common sense of honor based upon and reinforced by shared conventions . . . (t)his shared status culture aids group efforts to monopolize for the group as a whole scarce social, economic, and cultural resources by providing coherence to existing social networks and facilitating the development of co-membership, respect, and affection out of which new networks are constructed. (DiMaggio, 1982, p. 189)

We contend here that an inherent cultural capital predisposes one to more remarkable development, as seen, for example, through improved social mobilities. The capacity to access institutions that can foster and improve one's technical knowledge, for instance, through schools or other training programs, gives individuals an advantage in the labor market. Similarly, graduates of elite institutions might have an edge in salary differentials (see Chevalier and Conlon, 2003). Entrance to such elite institutions would likewise require the acquired cultural reproduction. Individuals with the "right" background are more easily able to gain access to these, reflecting the thoughts similarly espoused by Freire's education politics (see Freire, 1985). Taking the example of how universities overseas that require applicants to obtain a specific English language proficiency score would, at the onset, disadvantage applicants who are unable to acquire such language proficiency in the first place. This argument relates to the issue discussed earlier, where the desire for uniformity and standardization pushes for the use of *the* language for more accessible communications. This can range from a national standpoint where one language is preferred over others, characteristic of but not limited to multi-ethnic and multilingual societies, to issues bordering a global consensus, such as the choice of English as the language for modernity. Similarly, policies that maintain this supposed cultural capital control may influence developments at different levels. For example, motivations that shape national policies such as the switching and reswitching of the language of instruction (English to *Bahasa Melayu*) for Science and Mathematics in schools in Malaysia. Such motivations may be attributed by the government to improve teaching and learning in schools but are not discounted by observers as stroking to the political acceptance of the Malay majority of the population (Gill, 2012). Deficiencies in the English language, which is alleged to be the language for modernity, are also seen in the younger generations due to this advertent language switch (Azmi, Hashim, and Yusoff, 2018). Similarly, as will be highlighted in this book, standardizations through language-in-education policies such as the bilingual education and MTB-MLE policies in the Philippines are related to the supposed better learning and the broader sociocultural manifestation of language in the country.

Looking at language as a patterned activity, Bernstein (1971) investigated the link between social class and language/speech, investigating the role of schooling in forming a social identity as influenced by communications in school. He argues the possibility of the cultural discontinuity between the two different modes of communication at home and the school (especially to a working-class child). The implication of this social development in schools features what we point out as the influence of language apart from pedagogy, where societal and cultural manifestations may be affected through the language used in educational institutions. This role of language in education can be seen through language policies set in the system. Language as a proxy for identity (Hintjens, 2008) is further elucidated in policies affecting essential social services. For example, the mother-tongue-based multilingual education (MTB-MLE) introduces the idea that the mother tongue is beneficial in understanding critical concepts required for learning (UNESCO, 2011). In this vein, the MTB-MLE was introduced in the Philippines in all public schools in 2012. This policy uses eight languages intending to improve learning in schools better. This also veers away from the dominant bilingual education policy of the country instituted in 1974. However, despite the display bought by the MTB-MLE policy, studies have pointed to this program as deficient, inundated by the lack of proper resources and extensive review of this policy (Monje et al., 2019). On the other side, the rising use of English as the preferred language in schools (Brock-Utne and Hopson, 2005) shows the tread to standardization as earlier described. Samuelson and Freedman (2010) notes that nations ranging from newly established, developing, and developed have advanced the use of English in their education language policies. While they point out the use of English as a political motivation in war-torn Rwanda, they also note how language education policies across Africa have instigated the use of English as a medium of content instruction in schools (ibid, p. 202).

As drawn above in rough, the link of language to development shows the tendency of policy formations to affect basic social services. In this instance, we talk about the role of language in education, where a preference for a particular language predisposes an individual's social mobility prospects. Those with the inherent cultural background might find it easier to achieve success in schools (and eventually the workplace), given their acquisition of a specific language, which might be missing from others. Similarly, political motivations that drive national policies might put forward advantages for a certain group over another. We contend that language is a significant part of socialization and cultural transmission, and policies that define language use and practice in countries can have a considerable effect on its population (see Mufwene 2010). Given the complexity of sociocultural and political dynamics of language use and practice, we hope to draw and contextualize the use of language and education in the Philippines as it links to the different issues affecting it.

Chapter 3

Language and National Identity

INTRODUCTION

Education plays a vital role in promoting the local or ethnic languages, national language, official language, and international language. These languages have different roles reflected in the Philippines' language policy; however, they have similar goals to enhance students' local and global communication ability. Introducing those languages in the education system helps students develop a sense of belonging and national identity.

This chapter reviews the roles of education and language in identity formation while contextualizing the significant policies discussed in Chapter 4. Issues relating to the Philippine languages, English language education in the Philippines, the Philippine English, and Mother-Tongue Based (MTB) education are examined to see how these policies impact the dynamics of identity formation.

This chapter also highlights specific issues in language and identity and national identity formation.

THE PHILIPPINE LANGUAGES

The Philippines is a multicultural and multilingual country with 106.7 million people in 2015 (PSA, n.d.). Historically, Filipinos are of Austronesian descent who migrated to the Philippine Islands during the Iron Age. People in the Philippines are called Filipinos who belong to different ethnic groups. Many of them are labeled as Cebuano, Tagalog, Ilocano, Hiligaynon, Central Bicolano, Waray, Kapampangan, Albay Bicolano, Pangasinan, Maranao, Maguindanao, Tausug, and Masbateño (Census, 2010). These various ethnic groups reside in Luzon, Visayas, and Mindanao, which are classified further into different regions. The 18 regions consist of the National Capital Region (NCR), Cordillera Administrative Region (CAR), Ilocos Region (Region 1),

Cagayan Valley (Region 2), Central Luzon (Region 3), Calabarzon (Region 4), Southwestern Tagalog Region (Mimaropa), Bicol Region (Region 5), Western Visayas (Region 6), Central Visayas (Region 8), Zamboanga Peninsula (Region 9), Northern Mindanao (Region 10), Davao Region (Region 11), Soccsksargen (Region 12), Caraga (Region 13), Bangsamoro (Bangsamoro) (PSA, 2021).

The Philippines is an archipelago consisting of more than 7,100 islands located in Southeast Asia with 181 living languages (Dayag, 2016; Campesino and Telen, 2014; Lewis et al., 2014). Except for the Chavacano, a Spanish creole spoken primarily on the Zamboanga Peninsula in Mindanao, all indigenous languages in the Philippines are Austronesian (Paz, 1995). Generally, the Philippine languages belong to the Western Malayo-Polynesian group, the Malayo-Polynesian branch of the Austronesian language family (Lobel, 2000).

Across the country, there are at least eight significant languages with a considerable number of native speakers. These languages are Tagalog, Ilocano, Bicol, Kapampangan, Pangasinense, Cebuano, Hiligaynon, and Waray. Tagalog, Cebuano, and Ilokano are extensively studied (Abastillas, 2015), while the minor languages are not studied widely and are still unexplored up to this time. Ethnic diversity reflects the diverse linguistic backgrounds of the country.

Filipino is the national language, and both Filipino and English are the official languages. In the past, the Philippine bilingual language policy highlighted the importance of Filipino and English as Medium of Instruction (MOI) (Burton, 2003). However, some local languages in the Philippines are currently used as MOI in teaching the primary school children from grades 1 to 3. The Aklanon, Bikol, Cebuano, Chavacano, Hiligaynon, Ibanag, Ilocano, Ivatan, Kapampangan, Kinaray-a, Maguindanao, Maranao, Pangasinan, Sambal, Surigaonon, Tagalog, Tausug, Waray, and Yakan are the recognized local or regional languages in the Philippines permitted to be used as MOI by the Department of Education under the Mother Tongue-Based Multilingual Education (MTB-MLE) (Burton, 2003). Apart from the regional languages and the national language, English is also widely used in the Philippines.

The next section of this chapter provides a piece of background information about the status of English in the Philippines.

ENGLISH LANGUAGE IN THE PHILIPPINES

English is the de facto international language for international communication. The dominance of English today causes linguistic inequality and a feeling of anxiety and insecurity in those who cannot speak the language in a rapidly globalizing world (Tsuda, 2008). Realistically, English gains its dominance over other languages and plays a crucial role in promoting globalization. Therefore, the ability to communicate in English is now a necessity for everyone. It has become the language of the global village and serves as a neutral language to people who come from different linguistic backgrounds. At present, people who can communicate English fluently always have an edge locally and internationally. It has become the language of power and prestige, thus acting as a social gatekeeper to social and economic progress (Pennycook, 2017). This is why the Philippines gives importance to English because it becomes a pathway toward economic progress and better learning opportunities (Madrunio et al., 2016).

"English is the world's dominant language because it has 1.5 billion speakers, designated as official languages in more than 62 nations, the most dominant language in scientific communication, the de facto official and working language in most international organizations, and the most taught foreign language across the world" (Ammon, 2001, p. v; Jenkins, 2015). The English language serves as a common medium for international and intercultural communication in a global society.

In the Philippines, English and Filipino are the commonly used languages in many formal domains of communication. Despite the declaration of Filipino as the national language, English still plays a significant role because of its broader social function in education, government, and business. English in the Philippines is essential for economic reasons, and studies show that English proficiency has become a job requirement for many companies, particularly when dealing with international clients and partners (Madrunio et al., 2016). "English is also used as a social stratifier that enables economic advancement, and the feature of English-competent society where political-economic elites usually emerge" (Tupas, 2003, p. 2).

The Philippines is recognized as one of the largest English-speaking countries in Asia and continues its role in educating more Filipinos to produce better English-speaking graduates. English has always been placed on a top priority of the Philippine education system, as reflected in the country's education language policy.

The Philippine education language policy has undergone some changes and development from the Bilingual Education Policy (BEP) to the Mother-Tongue Based Multilingual Education (MTB-MLE). Despite the language policy changes, English remains one of the most critical languages for educational purposes. BEP emphasized the importance of English and Filipino and used as MOI starting from primary up to tertiary education. However, on May 15, 2013, a significant change occurred after the Republic Act 10533, known as the Enhanced Basic Education Act of 2013 (RA 10533; sec. 2–3), was signed into law where MTB-MLE was also implemented and introduced the mother tongue as MOI from grade 1 to grade 3. However, starting from grade 4 onward, English and Filipino languages are taught and used as the media of instruction (Leaño et al., 2019). Using the mother tongue as MOI during the formative years enhances the children's proficiency in their first language and strengthens their ethnic identity (Schluessel, 2010).

LANGUAGE AND IDENTITY

Language always co-exists with identity, and it constructs and reconstructs the speakers' individual or group identities. According to Djite (2006,p. 6), identity refers to the "everyday word for people's sense of who they are as an individual or as a member of a group." Identity is something inherent that can be expressed individually or collectively through language (Kroskrity, 2000). It is a linguistic construction that represents the notion of who we are and also a means for others' expectations of the way we must be (Spolsky, 1999). Bauman (2000) argues that identity is a linguistic construct, which means that linguistic performances are the loci in which identity is constructed. Speakers may use a language naturally or intentionally, and it can be assumed that identity can be constructed consciously or unconsciously. Dumanig (2010) argued that the conscious negotiation of identity is a deliberate process of personal and group membership portrayal, while the unconscious negotiation of identity is a portrayal of one's identity defined by the person's overall experiences.

Identity is constructed individually through religious practices, names, naming practices, and rituals and constructed as group identity representation (Thomas et al., 2004). The speaker's identity represents the speech community or religious groups that a person belongs to. Such identity is obvious because of cultural and linguistic variations, including religious practices, stylistic variation, and language choice.

Blommaert (2005) further described the concept of identity that who and what you are is dependent on the context, occasion, and purpose. It could be understood that the construction of identity in every human activity becomes a part of everyday life. The daily rituals involving language use happen in the way people interact with each other, how people dress, how people act, how people write, and how they project themselves to others. Blommaert (2005) further illustrated that identity involves many things that could be described as a semiotic representation process that includes symbols, narratives, and textual genres.

It is also believed that identity has to be enacted and performed to be socially salient (Blommaert, 2005). As a result, people tend to label themselves and others as religious, fanatics, friendly, kind, and helpful as their identity markers. However, whether on an individual, social, or institutional level, identity is something that we are constantly building and negotiating throughout our lives through our interaction with others (Thornborrow, 2004). Every time people interact with others, they frequently negotiate their identities or multiple identities in one speech event because they are concerned about how others may perceive them (Goffman, 2007). Emphasis on identities is not essentially given, but it is actively produced through deliberate, strategic manipulation or out-of-awareness practices (Kroskrity, 2000).

A critical aspect of studying identity construction is the speaker's speech community, which contributes to establishing the speaker's identity. The term speech community is defined as the shared dimension related to how members of the group use, value, or interpret the language (Saville-Troike, 2003). Therefore, the group and individual identity could be established within the speech community membership. The community of practice can be recognizable through the speaker's use of the lexical items and the speaker's manner of speaking.

The construction of either individual or group identity can be explained clearly by Self-Categorization Theory. This theory explains how identity is constructed or reconstructed through language use.

Self-Categorization Theory

Self-Categorization Theory (SCT) believes that identity is constructed or formed through self-categorization. SCT aims to describe and explain the specific nature of relationships between the self, social norms, and the social context (Stets and Burke, 2000). The theory originated from Social Identity Theory (SIT), which argues that social identity refers to a person's understanding of the group or social category where he or she belongs (Stets and Burke, 2000). It also postulates that "individuals can categorize themselves as group members, and consequently, they act similarly with other members with a common identity, group orientation, and behavior" (Turner, 1991, p. 155; Turner and Onorato, 1999). This means that social influence contributes to the process of self-categorization because the way individuals categorize themselves is based on their social and group membership. According to Turner and Onorato (1999, p. 20), "the process of self-categorization results in self-stereotyping as well as depersonalization."

In self-categorization, the individual accentuates by emphasizing the self and group differences. In each categorization, the concept of self comes from the perception of similarities and differences between classes of stimuli (Turner et al., 1987). According to Turner and Onorato (1999) and Mummendey and Otten (2001), the individual's social and personal identities represent various self-categorization levels. Personal identity is directly dependent on one's social identity. This is why people of the same group affiliation can specifically identify who they are and how they differ from the other members. This means that the personal level of self-categorization occurs by emphasizing the intra-group similarities and differences.

Consequently, through the common group orientations, personal and individual differences are achieved and evaluated. Similarly, social identity is also influenced by personal and individual distinctiveness because they are the product of various intergroup and interpersonal differences (Turner and Oakes, 1989). At the social level, self-categorization accentuates the similarities and differences between the ingroup and the outgroup. As a result, the social group comparison may lead to stereotyping one group to another when social identity becomes more apparent than that of the personal identity; such a process is known as depersonalization of the self. Depersonalization is described as the possibility to perceive increased identity between self and ingroup members and difference from outgroup members, to perceive oneself more as the identical representation of a social category and less as a unique personality defined by one's personal differences from other ingroup members (Turner and Oakes, 1989, p. 245). Consequently, self-categorization of the social self enhances the group behavior due to the commonalities of their collective self-concept, which is transformed into collective self-interests (Mummendey and Otten, 2001; Turner and Onorato, 1999; Turner, 1991). In general, self-categorization is believed to provide the primary source for people's social orientation toward others.

This theory may help explain how people categorize their identity based on the language that they speak. In a multilingual society like the Philippines, where the mother tongue, Filipino, and English, are used as MOI, people construct the local and global identities. The use of the mother tongue, the national language, and the Philippine variety of English reflects the local identity of Filipinos while English reflects their global identity.

English Language Education

English is undeniably one of the widely spoken languages worldwide. Its development has become phenomenal, where several varieties have emerged as highlighted in World Englishes and Global Englishes. The varieties of English have become the identity markers of different English speakers.

Many non-native speakers believe that English language carries the native speakers' identity (Lawrence, 2020). Therefore, learning English as a Second language or as a Foreign language is linked to the native speakers' culture and identity (Edwards, 2009; Norton, 2009). This means that when learners speak a second or a foreign language, they also alter their identities and possibly conform to native speakers' identities. Such a notion may have been true to understand when and how the English language is used, leading to a better pragmatic understanding of the language. However, when English became widespread in various parts of the world and gained an international status, other English speakers started to use it as a means for local and global communication. Eventually, English has been integrated into the education language policies in multilingual countries like the Philippines, Singapore, Malaysia, and Oman.

In the Philippines, as mentioned earlier, English and Filipino are the official languages and used as MOI in various education levels (Dumanig et al., 2012). To further enhance the Filipino students' learning experience, the Mother-Tongue Based Multilingual Education (MTB-MLE) that goes together with the government's K-12 program was introduced to replace the Bilingual Education Policy (BEP). The new policy highlights that the mother tongue must be taught and used as MOI starting from grades 1 until grade 3, while Filipino and English are used as MOI starting from grade 4 onward. Despite the emphasis on the mother tongue still, English plays an essential role in education, business, and other formal transactions in the Philippines (Ocampo, 2017).

The English language education led to the development of English in the Philippines and has resulted in several first and second speakers of English (Martin, 2020). As English develops, it becomes a legitimate language variety, and Filipinos start to recognize it as Philippine English. Some local words and phrases from Philippine languages have been nativized to English. A study conducted by David and Dumanig (2008) showed that local languages in the Philippines have been integrated into their nativized Philippine English variety termed as basilect, mesolect, and acrolect. Through continuous research among local and international scholars, Philippine English became a standard variety of English. The Philippine Standard English is labeled as PE, and the non-standard variety is labeled as Taglish, a combination of Tagalog and English, commonly used in informal spoken and written discourses. Philippine English is a distinct variety and has become an indicator of Filipino identity and a salient marker of the speakers' nationality.

Philippine English and Filipino Identity

English language education in the Philippines focuses on developing the language proficiency of the graduates. One of the objectives of teaching English in the Philippines is to produce employable graduates. This means that graduates are expected to be proficient in English in oral and written discourses. Proficiency in English will help learners achieve good academic records in schools because it is used as MOI in public and private institutions. As a result, proficient speakers enjoy more benefits, and in contrast, less proficient speakers are somewhat disadvantaged. English language proficiency is usually associated with the speakers' education. Proficient speakers of English are perceived to have finished higher education degrees.

The Philippine English language variety is uniquely Filipino in its lexicon, structure, and pronunciation (Dumanig et al., 2020). With the emergence of the variety of English in the Philippines and its continuous development, Philippine English has become a national identity marker for Filipinos (Axel, 2011).

Bolton and Butler (2004) examined the dictionaries and stratification of vocabularies resulting in new lexicography for Philippine English (PE). Webster's unabridged dictionary has included some Anglicized Filipino lexis commonly used in education and the media. Consequenlty, Bautista (2001) examined college and university professors' attitudes toward Philippine English lexical items. The study revealed that college and university professors and students support the Philippine English vocabulary, although Standard American English seems to be more preferred among educators. The acceptance of the Philippine English has contributed to the Philippine English dictionary. Bautista and Butler (2000) published the *Anvil-Macquarie Dictionary of Philippine English for Secondary School* to create a national dictionary of Philippine English. The dictionary included some Philippine English words like *academician, bagoong, balut, bed spacer, blowout, comfort room, hold upper, Lechon, Taglish, viand,* and *Yaya*. Many vocabulary words in Philippine English do not exist in other Englishes. These words are uniquely Filipino that are widely used and accepted in the Philippine context. The lexical items might differ from other Englishes; however, they can be understood clearly if used and spoken in appropriate context.

Below are some of the Philippine English words included in the Anvil-Macquarie Dictionary of Philippine English vocabulary.

> Bedspacer - a person, usually a college student, who pays rent for the use of a bed in a private home
> Blowout - taking several people out to a restaurant and paying for everybody
> C.R. (Comfort Room) - toilet, bathroom
> Dine-in - "eat in," "for here"
> Gimmick - a planned or unplanned night out with friends
> Hostess - a prostitute
> Jeepney mass transit trams originally made from U.S. military jeeps
> Metro Aid - refers to public street cleaners or broom sweepers
> Officemate - a co-worker
> Parlor - hair salon, i.e., beauty parlor = beauty salon
> Rubber shoes - sneakers or athletic shoes

Salvage - a slang word for summary execution. The meaning evolved from frequent usage in sentences such as 'The corpse was salvaged from the Pasig River,' from the actual meaning: recovered or found.
Adapted from Bautista and Butler (2000).

The phonology of Philippine English lexical items is also distinct and slightly resembles the North American variant. Philippine English uses the rhotic accent, but there is a wide variation according to speakers' location and first language. Since many English phonemes are not found in most Philippine languages, pronunciation approximations are common, and they vary from one region to the other.

Some examples of non-native pronunciation include:

Filipino = [pili'pino] or [pʰili'pʰino]
Victor = [bik'tor]
Family = ['pɐmili] or ['pʰamili]
Varnish = ['barnis]
Fun = [pɐn] or [pʰan]
Vehicle = ['bɛhikel] or ['bɛhikol]
Lover = ['lɐber] or loob-er
Find = ['pɐjnd] or ['pʰɐjnd]
Very = ['bɛri] or ['bejri]

Adapted from Bautista and Butler (2000).

The phonetic transcriptions show the Filipino way of producing the Philippine English sound. However, the pronunciation shown above applies mainly in the Tagalog region, although a little similarity is shared with some other areas of the Philippines. Problems in producing [f], [v], and [z] sounds are common for some Tagalog speakers because these phonemes are absent in Tagalog but are present in some other indigenous languages (Dumanig, 2004). It should be noted that mispronunciation is caused by limited sound inventories in most Philippine languages as compared to English (Dumanig, 2004).

Philippine English nowadays is an indicator of Philippine national identity. English is no longer viewed as a colonial language but as a language of the Filipinos. A study conducted by Dumanig and David (2014) on *Miscommunication in Malaysian-Filipino Interactions: Intercultural Discourse in English* proved that Philippine English is a distinct variety and reflects the Filipino national identity. Some examples of interactions are presented below.

Philippine English is used in this example to show how distinct it is as compared to other Englishes. Example 1 illustrates how communication occurs when two speakers use similar lexical items but with two different meanings.

Example 1

> A Filipino (F) asked a Malaysian (M) about the toilet.
> 1. F: Where is the Comfort Room here?
> 2. M: Don't know.
> 3. F: I mean, toilet.
> 4. M: There. (pointing to the toilet)
> 5. F: Thank you.

Adapted from Dumanig and David (2014).

Example 1 shows the interactions between Filipino and Malaysian interlocutors where English is used. In turn 1, the Filipino speaker uses a Philippine English lexical item, "comfort room" to mean toilet, but the Malaysian interlocutor responded, "don't know" in turn 2, which Filipinos can perceive as an impolite response for not being helpful. However, Malaysians tend to say, "don't know" when they do not understand a message. However, in turn, 4, when the Filipino speaker self-repaired by saying, "I mean, toilet," then "M" was able to understand the message.

It is clear that using the euphemistic term, "comfort room," to describe a toilet led to misunderstanding. The use of "comfort room" could not be immediately associated with the lexical item, "toilet," by the Malaysian speaker. Therefore, a different meaning can be created, particularly using the lexis "comfort." Consequently, an unexpected response was made by the Malaysian speaker. However, the Filipino interlocutor realized that "comfort room" was not understood, then later replaced the word with "toilet." In the end, both speakers understood each other, and the Filipino interlocutor achieved the goal of reaching the toilet.

Educating the Filipinos of the new English varieties helps them understand the other reasons for learning English. Currently, most Filipinos think that English is taught and a requirement in the Philippine educational system because it is one of the country's official languages and a language for economic advancement (Madrunio et al., 2016). Many people believe that if graduates can effectively communicate in English, they can quickly find jobs or have better job opportunities (Dumanig et al., 2020).

Lexical Choice

The Philippine English variety has created an impact in constructing and reconstructing the Filipino identity. The distinct Filipino identity attached to the Philippine English variety is easily recognizable by many speakers of English. Such distinct characteristics may result in more cohesive interactions among Filipinos or create barriers in communication with those who are not familiar with Philippine English.

The use of Philippine English serves as identity markers and indicators of Filipinos' individual or collective identities. This happens because individuals may categorize themselves as members of a group because of their similarities (Turner, 1991; Turner and Onorato, 1999), and language can be one of those.

The interviews conducted with Filipinos working as domestic helpers (FDH) and Filipino Information Technology professionals (FIT) in Malaysia show that the Philippine English lexical items indexed a Filipino identity.

Before I thought that the words that I used in English are also used by other speakers of English, but every time I talked to my colleagues they say that they did not understand so I tried to check in the dictionary and I found that the words exist only in the Philippines. That's why the next time I used it, I told them that this is how we Filipinos speak English. (FIT 13)

My employer is Chinese. Both of them (referring to the couple) are pure Chinese, but they speak English with me, but most of the time, they speak Chinese at home. Every time I talk to them, they always tell me that my English is different and they sometimes don't understand, and they said I'm using words not found in English. They told me that my English is different, but I know my English is correct. I think they don't speak good English. (FDH 1)

Adapted from Dumanig et al. (2020).

Pronunciation

The Philippine English pronunciation is also another marker of identity. Such a distinct marker of Filipino identity is carried by them wherever they go. Most Filipinos do not speak English as their mother tongue; as a result, their English pronunciation differs from that of the native speakers of English. Some phonological differences in the production of vowels and consonants are evident when Filipinos speak. The phonological differences in Philippine English have played a role in constructing a Filipino identity. Filipinos are becoming aware of the phonological differences of Philippine English. In the interviews conducted, the participants said:

My boss corrects me most of the time and tells me that I pronounce the words wrongly. For example, I say "bag," and he says "beg." I think my pronunciation is right. (FDH 15)

I think our pronunciation is different because we follow American English. We are easily identified as Filipino with such pronunciation (FIT 4)

Adapted from Dumanig et al. (2020).

Accent

Apart from pronunciation, the accent is also a strong marker of identity. According to the Oxford Online Dictionary (2019), an accent is a distinctive way of pronouncing a language, especially one associated with a particular country, area, or social class. It also refers to the stress or emphasis that has to be placed on a letter in a particular word. The way we speak has an impact on the performance of our identity. Accent becomes a marker of the group identity of Filipino. The Filipino accent can be interpreted in many ways, and it can be a form of linguistic maintenance for them to be identified as Filipinos or a form of linguistic divergence.

In an interview conducted, the participants mentioned:

My co-workers identified me as Filipino because, from the way we speak, our accent is different from them. At first, I also find their accent different, but later I eventually change my accent. (FIT 15)

"By name, I am identified as Filipino, and also when I speak maybe my accent. My Malaysian, Chinese and Indian colleagues have also different accent. (FIT 8)

Adapted from Dumanig et al. (2020).

The English language in the Philippines is no longer perceived as foreign, but it is also considered as the language of Filipinos (Dayag, 2012). Such development and change of mindset are the product of English language education in the Philippines. Consequently, Philippine English has truly become a marker of Filipino identity and global identity.

Language Education and National Identity

MTB-MLE was implemented to enhance the ethnic identity of the Filipinos. The ability to speak the local languages creates a "sense of belonging," a feeling, belief, and expectation that one fits in the group and has a place there, a feeling of acceptance by the group, and willingness to sacrifice for the group (Macmillan and Chavis, 1986 as cited in Lampien et al., 2018). Furthermore, Hurtado and Carter (1997) defined "sense of belonging" as a psychological feeling of group members belonging to a social, cultural, or professional community. Such a feeling allows the members to feel that they are part of the community and develops their understanding of the "self" and "group membership."

In any group membership, language plays a crucial role. It allows members to communicate and interact appropriately with each other. Besides, language is the most visible marker that a person belongs to a particular group. MTB-MLE serves as a bridge to develop the students' sense of belonging, a feeling that they belong to an ethnic group that they should be proud of. The ethnic identity formation during the formative years may eventually enhance the sense of nationalism, which refers to people's love, loyalty, and devotion to a country. The sense of nationalism enhances the person's sense of belonging. One of the roles of education is to develop a sense of nationalism and national identity by emphasizing the country's culture, norms, practices, beliefs, religion, and language (Byung-Jin, 2003). Teaching students to know their ethnic roots will help them better understand who they are and their ethnic origins.

Introducing the national language and English from grade 4 onward equips students to understand the purpose of developing a national identity. Language is considered an essential requisite of national identity, and language use on a broader scope can be linked to identity construction (Villegas-Torres and Mora-Pablo, 2018). In a study conducted in Australia, Stokes (2017) argues that roughly two-thirds of 69percent of the public believes it is imperative to speak English to be a true Australian. This idea may hold true to Filipinos that to be a Filipino, you must speak Filipino because it serves as a national identity marker. Wodak et al. (1999) explained that national identity "is constructed and conveyed in the discourse, predominantly in narratives of national culture. National identity is thus the product of discourse" (p. 22). Moreover, Hh and Guo (2000) described national identity as how one identifies with the nation one belongs to, which is almost similar to the idea that "national identity as an essentially irrational psychological bond that binds fellow nationals together" (Connor, 1993, as cited in Allidou, 1998, p. 595). This means that language plays a vital role in the construction of group and national identities.

In search of better economic opportunities, many Filipinos travel to other countries as migrant workers. The Philippines is known as a global model for labor export and was the first labor-exporting country (Center for Migrant Advocacy (CMA), and Friedrich Ebert Stiftung Foundation (FES), 2009). Labor migration has contributed to the country's economic growth (Calzado, 2007) and has contributed to giving importance to English language education.

In the past, English has been viewed as the language of the colonizers, but later it becomes a language of the Filipino. Philippine English emerges as a variety of English spoken by Filipinos and a distinct language, different from other Englishes, associated with being a Filipino (Dumanig et al., 2020). Philippine English has its own lexical, grammatical, phonological, and pragmatic features and has become a Filipino national identity marker. Some lexical items that are used only by Filipinos are the word "viand" for dish, "comfort room (C.R.)" for toilet, and "board mate" for roommate. The variation of English is not only at the lexical level but more evident at the phonological level. For instance, the vowel "a" for "taxi, bag or bank" is produced as "a," there are occurrences of substitution between "f" and "p," and "v" and "b" (Dumanig and David, 2014).

Philippine English serves as a national identity marker for Filipinos and distinguishes them from other English speakers. Identifying themselves as Filipinos through the use of Philippine English enhances their group behavior because of the commonality of their self-concept (Turner, 1991; Turner and Onorato, 1999; Mummendey and Otten, 2001).

The language education policy in the Philippines serves a vital role in developing the Filipino identity. The language policy in the MTBL-MLE paved a way to promote the multicultural and multilingual nature of the country. Introducing the mother-tongue languages from grade 1 to grade 3 develops the ethnic identity and sense of belonging of the young Filipinos. The introduction of Filipino and English languages from grade 4 onward enhances identity formation and leads to a deeper understanding of the Filipino national identity.

Notes

Interview quotations republished with permission of Peter Lang Copyright AG, from "Miscommunication in Malaysian-Filipino Interactions: Intercultural Discourse in English," Dumanig, F., and David, M. K., In *English in Malaysia: Post-Colonial and Beyond*, Hajar Abdul Rahim and Shakila Abdul Manan (Eds.), pp. 251–76, 2014; permission conveyed through Copyright Clearance.

Interview quotations republished from Francisco Perlas Dumanig, Maya Khemlani David and Syed Abdul Manan (2020). "Transporting and Reconstructing Identities through Language Use in the Workplace: Focus on Filipinos in Malaysia." *Journal of Multilingual and Multicultural Development,* Taylor and Francis, DOI: 10.1080/01434632.2020.1845707, reprinted by permission of the publisher (Taylor & Francis Ltd, http://www.tandfonline.com).

Chapter 4

Language-in-Education Policies in the Philippines

INTRODUCTION

This chapter provides a review of the Philippines' main language policies from the Bilingual Education Policy (BEP) of 1974 to the Mother-Tongue-Based Multilingual Education (MTB-MLE) of 2012. The development and changes in the BEP and MTB-MLE are highlighted. This chapter also discusses the role of the English language in education policies and reform in the Philippines. The roles and related issues of BEP and MTB-MLE will also be reviewed, alongside educational reforms in the country.

PHILIPPINE EDUCATION: OVERVIEW

Before the Philippines attained complete independence in 1946, the country's education system was patterned on the systems of Spain and the USA. Spain colonized and governed the Philippines for more than three hundred years and the USA for 48 years. After the Philippines gained independence from the Americans, its education language policy has constantly undergone reforms; from the Bilingual Education Policy (BEP) to the Mother-Tongue-Based Multilingual Education (MTB-MLE).

During the pre-colonial period, most Filipino children were provided solely with vocational training supervised by parents, tribal tutors, or those assigned for specific, specialized roles within their communities. In most communities, stories, songs, poetry, dances, medicinal practices, and advice regarding all sorts of community life issues were passed from generation to generation, mostly through oral tradition. Some communities utilized a writing system known as "Baybayin," a pre-Hispanic Philippine script, which has wide and varied use, though other syllabi are used throughout the archipelago (Nebre, 2019).

During the Spanish period, in the sixteenth century, religious schools and universities were opened by the Augustinians, Franciscans, Jesuits, and the Dominicans, and the language used as MOI was Spanish. Education opportunities at that time were limited only to the elites. Poor Filipinos did not have access to education and had limited to no knowledge of the Spanish language. During this period, the Spanish established printing presses to print books in Spanish and Tagalog. The publications of books and other printed materials in both languages helped Filipinos learn the Spanish language in schools (Dawe, 2014).

As discussed in previous chapters, in the middle of the nineteenth century, the Educational Decree of 1863 paved the way for a free public school system in the Philippines. Through this decree, one primary school for boys and one primary school for girls was opened. The implementation of such a decree significantly increased the number of schools and students in the country.

During the American Period, particularly in the latter part of the nineteenth century, more schools were opened. An experimental public school system was implemented in 1901 by the Philippine Commission. During this time, hundreds of American teachers known as the Thomasites arrived in the Philippines. The Americans brought English to the Philippines and used it as MOI in schools. It was also during that time that the Philippine Normal School was established to train Filipino teachers.

Dawe (2014, p. 63) stated that "the use of English as the MOI during the American period was viewed to be more appropriate." According to William Howard Taft, the first governor-general to establish a civilian government in the Philippines.

> They [the Filipinos] would never learn individual liberty or the power of asserting it, and I am afraid they would continue to be separated from each other, shut out from the light of civilization by a continuance of the knowledge of the dialects only and of no common language, which would prevent their taking in modern ideas of popular government and individual liberty. One of our great hopes in elevating those people is to give them a common language, and that language is English, because through the English language certainly, by reading its literature, by becoming aware of the history of the English race, they will breathe in the spirit of Anglo-Saxon individualism. (Graff, 1969, p. 42)

After the Philippines gained independence from the Americans in 1946, Filipino was declared the national language to unify the Filipinos through a common language. It eventually became the MOI and was also declared as the official language along with English.

The next section highlights the country's education language policy, particularly the Bilingual Education Policy (BEP) and the Mother-Tongue-Based Multilingual Education (MTE-MLE) declaration.

BRIEF HISTORY OF THE PHILIPPINE EDUCATION AND THE CREATION OF THE LANGUAGE POLICY

This section will briefly trace the history of the Philippine education system from the pre-colonial period, the Spanish period, the American period, and the postcolonial period. The discussion also emphasizes the impact of Philippine independence on the education system, particularly on the language education policy. This section ends with a summary of the Bilingual Education Policy (BEP) and the Mother-Tongue-Based Multilingual Education (MTB-MLE).

In the sixteenth century, the Philippines was colonized by Spain and was ruled by Spain for more than 300 years. However, many Filipinos did not learn the Spanish language because Spain was reluctant to allow the Filipinos to learn the language (Casambre, 1982; Herrera, 2015). Despite the limited number of Filipinos who speak Spanish, some languages in the Philippines still greatly influence some languages. Many Filipino languages use the naming of months, days, numbers, streets, names of people, names of places, and names of celebrations or festivals mostly taken from the Spanish language. There are also places in Cavite and Zamboanga where until now, the Spanish Creole language is spoken. As discussed in Chapter 1, the Spanish built schools, colleges, and universities to educate the Filipinos using Spanish as the medium of instruction.

When the Americans defeated Spain during the Spanish-American war in 1898, the Philippines was sold to USA for 20 million US Dollars (USD) under the "Treaty of Paris" (Casambre, 1982; Herrera, 2015). The Philippines was under the Americans from 1898–1946, but the country was under American control from 1900 to 1942. In 1901, the Americans established the civil government under the leadership of William Howard Taft, the first American Governor-General of the Philippines. During this time, English was declared as the official language, and six hundred American teachers (Thomasites) were brought to the Philippines (Casambre, 1982).

During the American occupation in the Philippines, public schools were opened, and the first teachers were the Thomasites because they were on board with the USS *Thomas* when they were brought to the Philippines. When the English language became the official language, it was also used as the medium of instruction (MOI) in schools. The English language was eventually taught throughout the country, and some English words became part of the Filipino vocabulary. During the American period, a few schools were established, like the University of the Philippines, Philippine Normal College, and some Agricultural schools. Filipinos were introduced to Hollywood movies; American music like rock n roll, boogie, jazz; and games like table tennis, basketball, volleyball, boxing, and football. On July 4, 1946, the Philippines gained independence from the Americans.

Before the independence, on November 13, 1936, the Institute of National Language and later known as the *Surian ng Wikang Pambansa*, was first established. The said Institute was tasked to conduct a study and a survey to create a national language. Some regional representatives led by Jaime C. De Veyra and representative of Samar-Leyte-Visayans represent the Ilokano-speaking regions, the Cebu-Visayans, the Bikolanos, the Panay-Visayans, the languages of Filipino Muslims, and the Tagalogs (Aspillera, 1981). Some major languages in the Philippines had representatives.

On June 7, 1940, the Filipino language was declared as the national language and an official language of the Philippines, effective July 4, 1946 (Axel, 2011). With the declaration of the national language, which was based on the Tagalog language, opposition of other languages started to build in the Cebuano and Hiligaynon areas (Constantino, 1981).

In 1957, extensive research was conducted to explore the language that would be used as the medium of instruction to make Philippine education more relevant to the needs of the learners (Ramos, 1979). Later, the Board of National Education decided to implement the vernacular language as the medium of instruction in Grades 1 and 2. On the other hand, Pilipino (now Filipino) should be taught informally starting from grade 1, and more emphasis would be given onwards (Ramos, 1979). As far as English is concerned, it was taught as a subject in grade 1 and grade 2 and was used as MOI starting in grade 3. The vernacular was used as an auxiliary medium during the primary years, while in Secondary Education, Pilipino is used as the auxiliary medium (Ramos, 1979).

The implementation of the language policy in 1957 was unsuccessful, and the use of the vernacular, Pilipino, English, and Spanish was ineffective. Consequently, it led to the creation of the DECS Order No. 25, series 1974 about the Bilingual Education Policy (BEP) that Filipino and English should be used as the media of instruction (Constantino, 1981). Pilipino was used in Social Studies/Social Science, Work Education, Character Education, Music, Health and Physical Education, and the rest of the subjects were taught in English. Both Pilipino and English were also taught as subjects in primary and secondary schools.

In 1987, the 1974 Bilingual Education Policy changed the national language from "Pilipino" to "Filipino," as stated in Article XIV, Section 6 of the 1986 Philippine Constitution. It is stated in the Constitution as follows:

The national language of the Philippines is Filipino. As it evolves, it shall be further developed and enriched on the basis of existing Philippine and other languages. Subject to provisions of law and as the Congress may deem appropriate, the government shall take steps to initiate and sustain the use of Filipino as a medium of official communication and as a language of instruction in the educational system.

Moreover, Article XIV, Section 7 of the Philippine Constitution states that:

For purposes of communication and instruction, the official languages of the Philippines are Filipino and, until otherwise provided by law, English. The regional languages are the official auxiliary languages in the regions and shall serve as auxiliary media of instruction. Spanish and Arabic shall be promoted on a voluntary and optional basis.

The Bilingual Education Policy successfully promoted the Filipino language, developing the language proficiency of the national language among Filipino students, promoting the importance of the Filipino language, and developing English as a second language (Nical et al., 2003). On the other hand, the local languages were not given priority, and the language proficiency of many Filipinos in their first language or mother tongue started to decline. To revive the mother tongue and to enhance multilingualism in the country, MTB-MLE was proposed. UNICEF (1999, p. 41) also acknowledged that "there is ample research showing that students are quicker to learn to read and acquire other academic skills when first taught in their mother tongue. They also learn a second language more quickly than those initially taught to read in an unfamiliar language."

In less than ten years since its implementation in 2012, several studies have been conducted highlighting some of the major issues in teaching the mother tongue (Rosario et al., 2016). This includes the teachers' training and preparedness, availability of teaching materials, and learners' attitudes toward the mother tongue.

EDUCATION LANGUAGE POLICY IN THE PHILIPPINES

The Philippines has eight major languages: Tagalog, Cebuano, Ilokano, Hiligaynon, Bikol, Samar-Leyte, Kapampangan, and Pangasinan (Dumanig, 2010). During the Philippine independence, Filipino was declared as the national language in 1959. The Filipino language, based on the Tagalog language (introduced in the 1930s), is widely spoken in Manila and provinces of Rizal, Cavite, Laguna, Batangas, Quezon, Nueva Ecija, and part of Tarlac (Gonzalez, 1998).

As discussed in Chapter 2, the declaration of the Filipino as the national language brought some issues because of the comparable number of speakers of the Cebuano language. The accusations from the speakers of the Cebuano language (Visayas and Mindanao) that the choice of Filipino is a form of Tagalog imperialism or internal colonization resulted in a resolution of changing Pilipino to Filipino. In 1971, the issue of creating a universalist approach in naming the national language and was to change Pilipino to Filipino to represent those Philippine languages with voiceless labiodental fricatives (Gonzalez, 1998). The change from "Pilipino" to "Filipino" was to make the national language more inclusive. Pilipino is associated with Tagalog, while "Filipino" is enriched with words from other local Philippine languages, which signal the non-exclusivist and multilingual character (Nolasco, 2010). The 1987 constitution stated that "Filipino" is the national language of the Philippines.

In light of the need to give importance to the vernacular language, a new policy in 1973 was implemented wherein the vernacular language was used as MOI in the primary level (i.e., grades 1 to 2). However, such an attempt was not successful, and the policy was revised by allowing English and Filipino as MOI in all levels and using the vernacular only as an auxiliary language (Bernabe, 1987; Llamzon, 1977). In 1974, the BEP was implemented, and in 2012, the MTB MLE was implemented to replace the BEP.

BILINGUAL EDUCATION POLICY (BEP)

The 1974 Bilingual Education Policy (BEP) of the Philippines, which was revised in 1987, stated that English and Filipino are the languages of education and the country's official languages. The implementation of the BEP aims to make Filipinos bilingual. Studies have shown that the BEP resulted in the abandonment of the minority languages in the Philippines (Grimes, 2000; Jernudd, 1999; Kaplan and Baldauf, 2003; Nical et al., 2003; Young, 2002).

With the introduction of the Bilingual Education Policy in 1970, the Pilipino language (later changed to Filipino) was used as MOI in the primary and elementary levels. On the other hand, the vernacular languages were used as MOI from grade 1 to grade 4 in the non-Tagalog speaking areas. The Filipino and English were introduced as double-period subjects from grade 5 to grade 6, and at the same time, both languages were used as MOI from grade 5 to Secondary School (Bernabe, 1987, p. 145).

In the revised policy, the vernacular languages have been used in government schools as "transitional languages" for initial instruction and early literacy up to primary grade 3, but these were carried out on a small scale. In this policy, local languages have been elevated to the role of "auxiliary languages." These local languages are used mostly to explain the curriculum to students and are not used seriously as the MOI. However, in some cases, local languages or multilingual learning materials are also used, which produced good results (Dumatog and Dekker, 2003). Situations vary depending on teachers and the availability of learning materials in local languages.

The BEP provides an opportunity to enhance and develop the national language, given the variety of languages in the Philippines. Additionally, there is a provision of English and regional languages in the educational system, though Filipino is still given much priority. Allowing other regional languages to be used as auxiliary languages, on the one hand, is also a good option because of the more expansive linguistic knowledge and proficiency of Filipinos in English and ethnic (regional) languages.

The Bilingual Education Policy states that

> Bilingual education in the Philippines is defined operationally as the separate use of Filipino and English as the media of instruction in specific subject areas. As embodied in the DECS Order No. 25, Filipino shall be used as a medium of instruction in social studies/social sciences, music, arts, physical education, home economics, practical arts, and character education. English, on the other hand, is allocated to science, mathematics, and technology subjects. The same subject allocation is provided in the 1987 Policy on Bilingual Education, disseminated through Department Order No. 52, s. 1987. (Espiritu, 2007)

The BEP aims to develop the students' competence in Filipino and English. It further aims to enhance learning through the use of the two languages to achieve quality education as called for by the 1987 Constitution, to propagate Filipino as a language of literacy, to develop the Filipino as a linguistic symbol of national unity and identity, and to cultivate the Filipino as a language of scholarly discourse (Espiritu, 2007).

With the overall emphasis on two languages, Filipino and English, the importance and role of other vernacular languages started to have diminished. Many minority language speakers have developed a more positive attitude toward English or Filipino for political, social, and economic reasons. Unfortunately, more negative attitudes are created toward the vernacular languages because of their lower status and limited functions in society (Obiols, 2000).

As a result, the new generation of speakers slowly abandoned some minority languages, such as the Butuanon language, a member of the Visayan dialect family, and Cuyonon language, a member of the Malayo-Polynesian languages spoken mainly in the Cuyo Islands, Palawan (Eder, 2004). However, it should be mentioned some well-established majority languages like Cebuano, Ilokano, and Ilongo have not been as much affected as other minority languages. As the writing systems for most languages are fairly similar in the Philippines, many people literate in Filipino can often quite easily transfer their literacy skills into their mother tongue (Jernudd, 1999; Young, 2002).

The demand for the English language is supported by various stakeholders, given that its acquisition would mean better opportunities for job securement, both locally and overseas. The massive migration of skilled and unskilled workers from the Philippines is documented by the 35 billion US Dollars workers' remittances and compensation of employees in 2020 (Remittances, 2021). This explains why institutions offering training in English are favored by the general public and draws in rough how the Filipino language is advocated to develop a stronger sense of nationalism while preference is given to the English language by most, given its ability to open doors for better opportunities.

After several years of implementing the Bilingual Education Policy, a new education language policy, the Mother-Tongue Based Multilingual Education (MTB-MLE), was implemented in 2012.

MOTHER-TONGUE-BASED MULTILINGUAL EDUCATION (MTB-MLE)

The Philippine government had shifted back to the promotion of the vernacular/mother tongue (not necessarily Filipino given the variety of languages/dialects in the Philippines) in schools when the Department of Education (DepEd) institutionalized the Multilingual Education (MLE) initiative in 2009 aiming to promote the use of the mother tongue or first language over the second language, to promote better learning among the students. Studies show that using the mother tongue as a medium of instruction may easily facilitate better learning (Chimbutane, 2011; Chimbutane and Benson, 2012; Trudell, 2007). The government believes that students will learn better if such a multilingual approach is applied. Under this scheme, two languages for instruction are used, and policy enactment stems from the Lingua Franca Education Project (LFEP) results of 1999 and the Lubuagan First Language Component (Walter and Dekker, 2011).

The LFEP was an experimental project for grade 1 students (age 7), which aimed at that time to "define and implement a national bridging program from the vernacular to Filipino and later English to develop initial literacy for use in public schools" (DECS Memo 144, p. 1). The policy was fully implemented in 2012 in all public schools, with emphasis given to kindergarten and grades 1 to 3 levels (i.e., ages 5 to 9). This policy is also in line with the Department of Education's policy of "every child a reader and a write by grade 1." About 900 schools, including those with indigenous peoples, have been modeling the MTB-MLE prior to the full implementation order of 2012, which used eight languages in the roll-out. It should be noted that the Philippines is a multiethnic/lingual country, so the mother tongue in this sense is not necessarily the Filipino language (i.e., the National language).

MTB-MLE focuses on "the effective use of more than two languages for literacy and instruction" (DepEd, 2016). Studies have proven that MTB-MLE brings more advantages to learners. Cabansag (2016, p. 43) highlighted the benefits of adopting the MTB-MLE enhances scholastic capability (Cummins, 2000; Thomas and Collier, 1997; Walter and Dekker, 2011); allows students to be actively involved in class (Benson, 2000; Dutcher, 1995); provides ease in accessing instructions (Benson, 2004; Smits et al., 2008); and improves the analytical and critical thinking of students (Brock-Utne, 2014).

The MTB-MLE is featured in two modes: (a) as a medium of instruction and (b) as a learning subject/school course. It further states that:

> The learners' mother tongue (L1) shall be used as the medium of instruction (MOI) in all domains/learning areas from Kindergarten through Grade 3 except [for school subjects] Filipino (L2) and English (L3). The L1 will continuously be used as MOI in a transition or bridging process through (L1-L2-L1 or L2-L1-L2) Grade 3. The L2 will be introduced in the first semester of Grade 1 (. . .) and continuously developed from Grades 2–6. Oral fluency in L3 will be introduced in the 2nd semester of Grade 1 (. . .) [other] macro-skills will be developed starting 2nd semester of Grade 2 until 6. (DepEd Order 16, p. 3)

Although there should be a better balance in using English and Filipino as MOI to cultivate a balanced bilingual speaker, studies reveal that sometimes the policy does not translate to the actual classroom practice. There is an evident mismatch between the language policy and the actual classroom practices where learners and teachers give more priority to English than Filipino (Dumanig et al., 2012). This is undeniable since English remains an influential language in the country, which highly impacts education and economic advancement (Koo, 2008). Bernardo (2004) emphasized that English serves as the language of power, upward mobility, and global communication and competitiveness in the Philippine context. Despite the benefits that English brings, it can have damaging effects on Filipino culture because it might result in less chance or motivation for learners to learn Filipino (Koo, 2008) and their ethnic languages. MTB--MLE may help young learners develop a more profound sense of ethnic identity and fluency of the ethnic language. Besides, the mother-tongue's language proficiency might contribute to better interactions between young and old generations. Learning the mother tongue may develop a sense of pride in the learners' own language and ethnic group identity. The mother-tongue education raises awareness of young generations' language, culture, and identity. Studies have shown that it helps to develop the L1 proficiency of young learners, as reflected in the Department of Education report on the performance per mother tongue of grade 3 pupils (Ocampo, 2017).

MTB-MLE offers advantages to enhance the proficiency of students' mother-tongue languages, but it also poses several challenges to both teachers and students. The issues in the implementation of the BEP and the MTB-MLE are discussed in the next section.

ISSUES IN BILINGUAL EDUCATION POLICY (BEP)

The bilingual education policy in the Philippines helps promote the national language and instills a sense of Filipino national identity. The Philippines gives importance to its national language as exemplified, among others, in the inclusion of an annual nationwide celebration of *"Linggo ng Wika"* (Language Week) in schools to instill in students the significance of the national language for development.

The BEP emphasizes the use of English and Filipino as MOI; however, the Sections in the 1987 Constitution are not evident in practice in some educational institutions (basic to higher education levels). English is widely used and preferred on campuses despite the top-down language policy in the Philippines, which clearly advocates promoting and preserving the Filipino language. The 1987 Constitution (Article 14 Section 9) states that "the Congress shall establish a national language commission . . . for the development, propagation, and preservation of Filipino and other languages." Countervailing the *"Linggo ng Wika"* celebration is the 'Speak English" campaign in schools. Instead of enhancing the Filipino language in schools, English appears to dominate. A mismatch between policy and practice is documented (Gonzalez, 2003). Despite the clear mandate of the Filipino language as the official language of instruction in educational institutions, its subordinate status compared to the English language is apparent (Durano, 2009).

However, some pursue the use of the English language as means to act as a tool for "interconnectedness" as constructed colonialism (Pennycook, 1998). As discussed in Chapter 3, English is used as a social stratifier that enables economic advancement (Tupas, 2003), all draw above in rough the colonial and imperialist feature of the language still advocated by some (Obondo, 2007). The line of reasoning that development and nationalism cannot "go together," though rather sweeping, was argued by Sta. Maria (1999, 85) that the Philippines must "set aside at this critical period of our development . . .

over-zealous feelings of nationalism, which deter our efforts at improving the teaching of English." This usual measure of nationalism to language use during the debate of the bilingual policy, however, now has been taken over by an overriding theme that cognitive development improves significantly if the first language is used in instruction, with the sociocultural aspect of national pride evidently still emphasized in the discourse but not necessarily taking precedence. Despite the increasing call to internationalize and the move toward promoting the English language in the country, advocates of the effectiveness of using the mother tongue as MOI for schools are now reviving the call to promote the "local" language. The institutionalization of the mother tongue-based multilingual education (MLE) reflects this, notwithstanding the costs to be incurred for promoting such a policy.

ISSUES IN THE MOTHER-TONGUE-BASED MULTILINGUAL EDUCATION (MTB-MLE)

The teaching of mother tongue is a big challenge to primary school teachers, although they are well-trained educators who completed a Bachelor's degree in Elementary Education and passed the Licensure Examination for Teachers (LET). Most teachers who have been teaching using the L1 (mother tongue) as MOI have minimal training and limited instructional materials in the mother tongue (Dumanig et al., 2012; Madrunio et al., 2016). Due to scanty instructional materials, teachers resort to translating English textbooks into the mother-tongue language (Dumanig et al., 2012). It has become a disadvantage to those who are teaching the mothertongue languages that are not widely studied and have very limited resources. However, some instructional materials are ready and prepared in some areas whose L1 has been studied and have already sufficient resources.

To maintain better output despite the issues on textbooks and teachers, schools implement a regular evaluation for teachers, like the classroom observations by the master teacher and school principal, to ensure the quality of teaching. Moreover, pupils are also evaluated by teachers through quizzes and quarterly examinations. If found that students do not have sufficient language skills in the mother tongue, they are given remedial classes, and parents are asked to get involved in the pupil's learning (Dumanig, 2019; Lartec et al., 2014).

The challenges in the implementation of MTB-MLE in primary school are the teachers' ability to teach L1 and the availability of instructional materials in 19 local languages (Eberhard, et al., 2020). The Philippines has 181 languages (Dayag, 2016; Campiseno and Telen, 2014; Lewis et al., 2013) spoken in various regions. Developing new instructional materials in local languages will require more research and a sizable amount of funding from the government. On the other hand, schools should provide more training to teachers who are teaching the mother tongue; otherwise, teachers' limited or haphazard training may not fully bring success in the implementation of MTB-MLE. Although continuous training was provided prior to MTB-MLE implementation, it was not sufficient, as Nolasco (2012) argued that hundreds of teachers were brought into weeklong camps and haphazardly trained by instructors who were not familiar with the concept of MTB-MLE. It only shows that teachers were not provided with the necessary training on how to teach the mother tongue, and it is necessary to retrain the teachers. A position paper was submitted in 2020 to the House Committee on Basic Education and Culture to abolish the MTB-MLE with the notion that students performed better when instructions were in English (Albano, 2020).

The other challenge is the perception of stakeholders on the importance of English (L3) as compared to the mother tongue (L1) and Filipino (L2). Despite the continuous effort to promote the mother tongue and at the same time enhance the young learners' knowledge of the national language (Filipino) and international language (English), it is still undeniable that many people in the Philippines have a higher preference for English language (L3) because it serves as a symbol of power and prestige (Tupas, 2008) apart from its educational and economic benefits (Dumanig et al., 2012; Madrunio et al., 2016; Nakahara, 2006).

These challenges in the implementation of MTB-MLE could be minimized or at least be resolved if the Department of Education will seriously take actions in developing more instructional materials in teaching the mother tongue, more training and retraining of primary school teachers, and creating awareness to stakeholders on the importance of L1 to enhance the learning of L2 and L3.

Although there should be a better balance in using English (L3) and Filipino (L2) as the MOI in order to cultivate a balanced bilingual speaker, studies reveal that sometimes the policy does not really translate to the actual classroom practice. As the policy states, there should be proper implementation of multilingual education to balance the students' learning. Emphasis on English is necessary because of its economic and social benefits. However, emphasizing the Filipino language in secondary classes is also essential to enhance the students' knowledge of the national language, which eventually develops their sense of nationalism and identity. Proficiency in the national language increases the learners' sense of Filipino identity.

If the use of English and Filipino as MOI and the mother tongue as an auxiliary in the lower and upper secondary levels is properly implemented, it could be effective in learning two languages and in learning other content subjects. Studies show that there is no evidence of any harmful effects of bilingual education, and using two languages as MOI has benefits in many domains (Bialystok, 2016; Vygotsky, 2012). In some cases, learners may use one language as a resource to understand another language (Yadav, 2014). This is revealed in the study of Launio (2015) in Tapaz National High School, Philippines, that using two languages, such as English (L3) and Hiligaynon (L1), in teaching Mathematics contributed to a better performance of students in learning Mathematics. It shows that the use of the mother tongue language (L1) as a supplement to English (L3) is useful to help learners comprehend some mathematical concepts better. This means that learners who have limited proficiency in English can learn the course content using their native language (Chin, 2015).

As Launio (2015) argued, using the local language to teach the mathematical concepts might help enhance the students' performance and will assist them learning English as a second language. Before the implementation of MTB-MLE, the results of the National Secondary Assessment Test (NSAT) reflect the Filipino students' performance in English and Mathematics. The examination results show the low performance of secondary students in English (Cruz, 2008). In 2000, the scores were considered low in Mathematics (50.17), Science (44.50), and English (48.75). In 2004, the results in Mathematics (46.20) and English (50.08) and in 2005, the results in Mathematics (50.70) and English (51.33) did not have any significant improvement (Cruz, 2008). That brings to the idea that perhaps the mother-tongue education might improve the students' performance in English, Mathematics, and Science. Due to such results on students' performance in Mathematics, Science, and English, the curriculum was revised in 2010 with the aim to improve the functional literacy of Filipino secondary graduates who can communicate and interact effectively in various contexts. To attain such an aim, the 2010 curriculum focused on various learning programs such as the Content-Based Instruction, CALLA (Cognitive Academic Language Approach), Problem-Based Education, Tasked Based Education, Competency-Based Approach (PTCBL) text-based and genre-based approach (Cunanan, 2012).

LANGUAGE EDUCATION REFORMS IN THE PHILIPPINES

Historically, Philippine language education underwent several reforms starting from the colonial period until today. With the aim to provide education to Filipinos, the role of language education has been given importance in the education system. During the colonial era, colonial languages such as Spanish and English were imposed as the media of instruction in schools. Even after gaining independence, after the Philippines declared Filipino as its national language, these two colonial languages were still influential in Philippine language education.

Prior to the implementation of MTB-MLE, the Bilingual Education Policy (BEP) was implemented in the 1970s, where Filipino and English were used as the media of instruction. Based on Republic Act No 10533, Sec. 4 states that the enhanced basic education program includes at least one (1) year of kindergarten education, six (6) years of elementary education, and six years of secondary education. During kindergarten and the first three (3) years of elementary education, the mother tongue is used as the MOI. As students continue to grade 4 until grade 6, Filipino and English are gradually introduced as languages of instruction until such time when these two (2) languages can become the primary languages of instruction in the secondary level.

As discussed in Chapter 3, giving importance to the Filipino languages helps promote the unity and identity of the Filipinos through language education while maintaining the English language proficiency for globalization. Moreover, BEP aims to achieve language competence in Filipino and English. On the other hand, the local or regional languages in the Philippines were used as auxiliary languages in lower primary grade levels (refer to Chapter 3).

Tupas and Martin (2016) argued that one accomplishment of BEP in the Philippines had been the insertion of Filipino in educational provision across all levels of schooling. This accomplishment enhances the Filipino identity through language. As emphasized in Self-categorization theory, the integration of the national language or some local languages as MOI in schools develops students' sense of belonging. The integration of the Filipino language as MOI may help intellectualize the national language. Sibayan (1991) argued that limiting the use of the English language through mathematics and science teaching helped to intellectualize the national language.

On the other hand, the BEP focused more on the two languages: Filipino and English. The policy somehow side-lined the country's multilingual and multicultural nature and the importance of the mother-tongue languages. Studies show that the minority students who gained literacy in their mother tongue or first language revealed a higher academic achievement than students who learned a second language (Ramirez et al., 1991; Thomas and Collier, 1997; Walter and Dekker, 2011). Other studies show that the second and third languages can be easily acquired if the learners had a good foundation in the first language (Ramirez et al., 1991; Thomas and Collier, 1997; Walter and Dekker, 2011).

Chapter 5

Education, Language Policy, and Use in the Philippines

INTRODUCTION

The rapid and increasing internationalization of services has now, more than ever, engaged the education sector with issues that delineate government policy orientations in response to the needs of the knowledge economy. From central points of access and the increasing democratization of education through the upsurge of information and communications technology (ICT) to equity issues that define the rights to education for all, education policies globally have set the tune to responding to the cultural and local needs of a society while ensuring at the same time, that its population is receptive to the demands of modern times. The role of language policy affecting education has been discussed in the literature (Tollefson, 2002; Meken and Garcia, 2010; Watson, 2011). From the rise of the English language as '"he" language for globalization to the call for a more inclusive and locally oriented mother-tongue-based multilingual education (MTB-MLE), this chapter will broadly discuss the dynamics of language, access, and influence. It will look at the Philippines as a country case study of explicit and implicit declarations in language policy and use as affecting the education sector and access to the labor market.

LANGUAGE, ACCESS, AND INFLUENCE

The role of language policy in democratic plurality is contentious given the functions exhibited by languages and power in nation-states, with postmodernists framing language as the core of political existence "steeped in power and defining people's role in the world" (Holborow, 1999, p. 1). The role of language in agency and power is marked, with agency defined as the "capacity to act" and with language as an integral part of agency (Woldemariam and Lanza, 2014). Realignment in language policies can also refer to changing political powers where "language education plays an important role in controlling access to economic resources, political institutions, and power (Tollefson 1993, 73). The realities of language and access are demonstrated further by Tollefson (1993, 1989) through his work on US education policies for South East Asian refugees. It contends that the education programs given to such groups limit their employment prospects rather than advancing it where their education advocates for "self-sufficiency" and channels them into "minimum-wage jobs that offer little opportunity for increasing language or job skills (p. 74). Nationalistic tendencies in language policy display similar concerns regarding access where a dominant and preferred language is used as a criterion for influence and control, as will be further discussed here.

Additionally, institutional narratives also play an essential role when often, such govern the "crucial purpose of legitimising specific language policies" (Rappa and Wee, 2006,p. 4). For instance, in Singapore, a member state of the Association of South East Asian Nations (ASEAN), whose lack of natural resources has compelled the State to develop and depend on its human capital for socioeconomic advancement. Given the ethnic background and diversity found in Singapore, the State has insinuated a bilingual proficiency where English (as the supposed medium for modernity) is widely used as a medium of instruction (MOI) in schools while at the same time, not discounting the role of ethnic languages identified by its population. On a similar note, neighboring Malaysia is placed, with as much ethnic diversity, as prioritizing the Malay language reflected in national policies such as the National Economic Policy (NEP) of 1970 and subsequent education language policy revisions. Notwithstanding contentions, such an outlook in language policy in Malaysia is clearly meant to privilege certain ethnic groups over others (Samuel and Tee, 2013; Phan, Kho, and Chng, 2013). Comparing the two countries follows how institutional narratives in language policy would influence the tread to effective modernization. It is seemingly more difficult for Malaysia to institute this given the footing of the Malay language over English.

Language policies as a factor in discriminating national ideologies are manifest though not necessarily the crux to successful national integration, as may be evident in Singapore where its younger population might not realize how "fragile inter-ethnic relations could prove to be . . . not having lived through poverty and deprivation (Tan, 2011, p. 164). Nonetheless, one cannot discount the commanding force of language in policy relations. Brunei Darussalam, also a member state of the ASEAN, has since established a bilingual education policy since 1985 in all government-run schools, while non-government-run schools were seen to adopt this plan voluntarily. The strong consensus to teach English in Brunei stems from the desire to be economically competitive, where English is considered the default medium for modernity in an increasingly globalized world. Comparably, the current influx of Korean students in the Philippines also speaks of the demand for the English language. The country is seen to have the competitive advantage in delivering quality training in the language in more "economical" terms than one would otherwise get from the West. This edge stems from the use of English as a working language in the Philippines which has also, as a result, seen a dramatic rise in the business process outsourcing (BPO) market in recent times. Such strides and predisposition to the English language are not limited to South East Asia. With the rising interconnectivity between and among societies and nations, this not only makes this "language of choice" more accessible but further strengthens the influence and command of English worldwide. Such impact was described by Fishman long ago to what is now perhaps the reality set by technologies and interconnectivity:

> The uniformizing requirements and consequences of technology are such that many monolingual nations in control of "old languages" will need to resort to diglossian compromises in various technological and educational domains for many years to come. (1968, p. 47)

Given the effects of mass urbanization, one cannot live in an entirely homogenous setting, where realities are now defined by multiculturalism and a multilingual world. The ideological and political use of a single dominant language in educational settings may be unattainable, given such and opens the debate on the written versus the spoken vernacular and issues in bilingual education (Hobsbawm, 1996). This ideal has also given impetus to the practice of mother-tongue-based multilingual education (MTB-MLE) especially documented in countries with a rich linguistic background. MTB-MLE advocates using the learners' first language or mother tongue as a medium of instruction in educational settings to promote supposed better quality in learning and offset the hegemony of certain languages that are seen to marginalize certain groups in societies. Tupas (2015) highlights the use of the MTB-MLE in two broad political contexts: (i) in educating linguistic minorities where a national or foreign language is employed as a medium of instruction and (ii) the practice of such policy in mainstream education displacing former languages used in education, while expounding on examples for the first case as relevant to Cambodia, Lao PDR, Myanmar, Thailand, and Vietnam; and the Philippines and Timor-Leste, on the other (p. 112). However, the MTB-MLE's quest for continuing influence is suspect in the ASEAN given its move for a more robust and more compact regional bloc through the ASEAN Economic Community (AEC) and with the predilection of using English as the working language under the AEC. Of course, there is also the increasing authority and impact of the English language, as abovementioned, in scientific and technological discourses.

ENGLISH: THE LANGUAGE OF CHOICE?

It is undeniable, the spread of English in the global setting is propelled further by the increasing internationalization of services worldwide. What was once hardly conceived as the international language with global dominance has now made its way to possibly every society imaginable. The 1966 Airlie House conference on Language Problems of the Developing Nations'considered English simply an option for "wider communication," far from the compelling force it is reckoned to be now (Spolsky, 2004). About a decade later, Fishman (1977) started to recognize the changing shift when he wrote the introduction of his book detailing the spread of English (as cited in Spolsky, 2004, p. 77):

> The traveler returning to the United States from a vacation trip in Africa, Europe, or Asia is often heard to comment that nearly everyone he met seemed to be able to speak some English. To such an impressionist account of the ubiquity of English as the world language.

More than two decades ago, the launch of the British Council's English 2000 project highlighted the already expanding and significant role of the English language in the international market: "Worldwide, there are over 1400 million people living in countries where English has official status. One out of five of the world's population speak English . . . English is the main language of books . . . international business and academic conferences, science technology." (Graddol 1997, p. 2)

The spread of English has taken in different angles, from Fishman''s (1977) interplay of various factors of, among others, education, political affinity, and urbanization, i.e., "making it happen," to Phillipson's polemic (1992, 2015) "linguistic imperialism" as a result of well-executed language management favoring the Centre while isolating and further relegating the Periphery into dependency. Phillipson argues this view as a form of linguicism, which he maintains as operating "through structures and ideologies and entailing unequal treatment for groups identified by language," comparable to racism and classism (Phillipson, 2015). Similar to other perceptions, this view of English as cultural imperialism defeats and questions the assumed and possible role of a "unifying" and "neutral" English when the language is considered as the primary bearer of Western economic hegemony (Pennycook,

1998; Holborow, 1999), and thus commonly viewed as a promoter of social inequality.

Nonetheless, the rise of English as a language of globalization and as the custodian of "fast capitalism" (Kress, 1995) has predisposed nations parallel to the economics of market demand to training its students and to studying the language in its own right, where articulacy in English is also equated to having better opportunities and self-advancement. Its rise in China, home to the world's largest population, and the European Union (EU) as one of the more established political-economic unions globally, reinstates further its already compelling influence in world communications. To the effect of it possibly having a role in promoting a world that is more equitable and ethically responsible (Johnson, 2009).

The role of language policies particularly affecting education has shifted to promoting English either as a second language, a working language, or adopting a bilingual education policy. However, implementation, management, and practice may not reflect the actual policy orientation. For instance, in Namibia, concerns have been raised of an ill-equipped setting where the language policy in education favoring English since 1990 faces the realities of lack of qualitative teacher training in the language. Results have been so damning which reveal that the majority of the teachers in the southern African state as not proficient in the language, where 70 percent of teachers in senior secondary schools are unable to read and write basic English, thus resulting in poor learning among students (Kitsing, 2012). Literature is also replete with the role of English side-stepping inherent cultural complexities of countries, where in some cases, advocates of mother-tongue-based multilingual education have called for a more inclusive setting by promoting this policy (Nolasco, 2008; Whitehead, 2013; Mustafa, 2015).

In South East Asia, the move toward a more integrated ASEAN, as discussed in previous chapters, has pushed for policy orientations in the region that dictate a more complementary and comprehensive approach toward development. For instance, the thrust toward great mobility through the Mutual Recognitions Arrangements (MRA) and the ASEAN University Network (AUN) highlight the role of greater standardizations and commodification in educational services. Mobility across countries in the ASEAN in terms of educational and job prospects equally demands using a standard '"ingua franca," setting the English language as the default choice of language. This need further underscores the role of English in globalization tendencies. The ability to acquire and master the language places an individual at an advantage in greater social mobility options. The choice of English in international communications in the ASEAN since its formation (though not formally adopted in 2009 as the region's working language) is contrasted against other organizations like the United Nations (UN), which have used several official languages (Okudaira, 1999). This unique consideration of English in official communications in the ASEAN has also provided advantages in saving of related translations costs and the push for "equality":

> The position of English in ASEAN is politically neutral. Each of the ASEAN member countries has provided its own "official language" on the national level. From this common ground, it has been solidly recognized in ASEAN that English is an "international language," not belonging to any particular country or culture but belonging to the "international community." One of the leading reasons why there has been no counter-argument in ASEAN against the use of English results from this perspective. (Okudaira 1999, p. 98)

National initiatives to push the English language within countries are also evident, as aforementioned, linked to the greater commodification of educational services. From Anglophone colonized countries such as the Philippines, Malaysia, Singapore, and Brunei, which have instituted bilingual policies (i.e., English and the national language) and English as a medium of instruction in schools. However, education reorientations during recent years have seen the rise of MTB-MLE in the Philippines, its possible implementation in Myanmar (McCormick, 2019), and reversals on the language of instruction in schools in Malaysia. While initiatives within the ASEAN were set some time ago in improving English language use for French-colonized countries through language assistance and training programs (Okudaira, 1999), current policies still mirror the desire to further the English language within populations. For instance, Vietnam's English 2020 policy aims to equip students with English language proficiency supported by the Ministry of Education and Training's (MOET) pilot testing of the English language curricula in schools (Hoang, 2018). The number of international development organizations in post-conflict Cambodia also requires its local graduates to know a working proficiency of English to secure jobs in such organizations (Kirkpatrick, 2012). But given the multilingual features of the ASEAN, it has been argued that pivoting to the English language puts other ethnic and local languages at risk (Kirkpatrick, 2012; Crocco and Bunwirat, 2014).

The following sections will discuss the rise and preference for the English language and the MTB-MLE as relevant in education language policies. While the latter is discussed more in detail in other chapters as it relates to identity formation, we interrogate this policy in line with the bilingual language policy of the Philippines as it relates to language preference and use in the country.

MOTHER-TONGUE-BASED MULTILINGUAL EDUCATION

The role of mother-tongue-based multilingual education (MTB-MLE) has been pushed in line with the desire to improve student learning, with the perception that using the mother tongue or first language of the child in early education will result in a better understanding of critical concepts needed in scholarship (UNESCO, 2011). Some advocates of the MTB-MLE also ruminate on the benefits to "access and inclusion" of this policy that will otherwise be lacking in schools administering a second or third language (not necessarily English) as its MOI. This alleged role in improved learning has resulted in critical debates and discussions in policy repositioning in both the national and international setting over the years. For instance, UNESCO's 1953 publication of *The Use of Vernacular Language Education* points to the sustained discussion of this, despite the recent resurgence of the MTB-MLE in education literature as a result for one, of the global call for universal education.

Notwithstanding the accolades bestowed upon the assumed merits of the MTB-MLE, issues of implementation and other executory difficulties may arise where there is a lack of teacher training in the language. Or when the language may not be written or if it is, resources are lacking (e.g., for reading, teaching) of the language (Spolsky, 2004). Tupas (2015) also discusses the predicament of ethnolinguistic minorities in Cambodia, Lao PDR, Thailand, and Vietnam in the quest to institutionalize the ideology of "one language, one culture, and one nation" (p. 117) while marginalizing other minority language groups. As exhibited in Pol Pot's obliteration of Cambodia: "In Kampuchea there is one nation and one language—the Khmer language. From now on, the various nationalities do not exist any longer in Kampuchea (Pol Pot as quoted in Edwards 1996, p. 55; Tupas 2015, p. 117).

In the Philippines, an explicit policy has been set on the MTB-MLE in consonance with intentions raised above, while other countries in South East Asia like Cambodia, Indonesia, Malaysia, Thailand, Timor-Leste, and Vietnam are piloting this initiative at the community level with support from international non-governmental (INGO) organizations (Burton, 2013). However, as the issue of language policy versus actual language practice and management often shows, the case of the Philippines' MTB-MLE shows discordance between a top-down policy and a community level practice, which will be discussed further in sections to follow.

LANGUAGE POLICY AND PRACTICE IN THE PHILIPPINES

Host to possibly one of the most extensive education sectors globally, the Philippines has over 62,000 schools (primary and secondary level) and over 21 million students enrolled in public schools alone (DepEd, 2015). The expanse of education is also seen in higher education. The year 2020 saw close to 2,400 higher education institutions (HEIs) in the country, with an estimated 3.4 million students enrolled in various HEIs (CHED, n.d. a). This trend highlights the continued massification and reliance on human resource development in the Philippines. While latest education initiatives such as the 2019 Transnational Higher Education law draws attention to the increasing push for greater mobilities and commodification of education in the country. The Philippines is also one of the more ethnically and linguistically diverse nations in South East Asia, represented by over a hundred ethnic groups and about 130 different languages, making language policy planning more challenging than usual. Recent initiatives by the Philippine government that aim to increase quality and access to education resulted in the institutionalization of the MTB-MLE in the country in 2009 and subsequently implemented in all public schools in 2012 (with eight major languages).

The MTB-MLE is also envisioned to support the "Every Child A Reader and A Writer by Grade 1" program, which is in line with the universal school participation target of the government. As discussed in other chapters, other language policy initiatives have also seen their influence in education and business-related matters in the country. For instance, through the Bilingual Language Policy (English and Filipino) of 1974, alongside the strengthening of the use of Filipino through the formation of the *Komisyon sa Wikang Filipino* (KWF) in 1991, and the Executive Order (EO) 335, which issued the use of Filipino in all government agencies' official communications. As we also described, the push for the use of Filipino does not go without contentions (see Chapter 2) and has also elicited similar protestations from the private sector: "English proficiency had declined considerably ... when Cory Aquino came to power, they insisted on using Filipino(... for nationalistic purposes which is stupid ... because English is the single most competitive edge we have compared to our neighbors" (Symaco, 2011, p. 151).

This explicit top-down approach to recognize the Filipino language has not similarly resonated in language practices, where people prefer the use of the English language with its association to be the "medium for modernity" (Dumanig, David, and Symaco, 2012).

> If I master the English language, I will have more chances of getting a job after graduation.
> If Filipino is given priority in school then I'll find another school that gives importance to English.
> I study to learn and to learn English so I can work abroad.
> Most companies hire applicants with good command of English.
> English is an international language and recognized all over the world, while Filipino is only used in the Philippines. (p. 108)

This mismatch is validated further by the KWF, which shows the limited use of the national language in higher education institutions in the country. The study points out the prevalent use of the English language in courses, publications, and research, given the familiarity of the lecturers with the language. The lack of Filipino terms and books in scientific settings also disadvantages the language over English (Geronimo, 2015). This mismatch stems despite the General Education Curriculum set by the Commission on Higher Education (CHED) in 1996 requiring tertiary students to enlist in 9 units of Filipino courses (for language and literature) and encouraging the Humanities and Social Sciences courses to be taught in Filipino, in consonance with the Bilingual Education Policy (CHED Memorandum Order 59, 1996).

Spolsky (2004) has highlighted the tripartite division of language policy into language belief and ideology and language practice (p. 39). Obviously, as in the case of the Philippines, the explicit language policies and plans meant to manage the language use and ideologies in the country have not gained the expected effect. A recent order by the CHED has been heavily criticized by Filipino language advocates when it revised the General Education Curriculum (for 2018) without any Filipino subjects. The *Tanggol Wika* (Save the Language) group has projected that more than 10,000 Filipino subject professors will be affected by the policy and the failure to instill nationalism among the students (Geronimo, 2014). This preference for English seen as the 'modern' language and its role as relevant to the labor market entry of the Filipinos will be examined in the section to follow.

ENGLISH FOR THE "GLOBALIZED" FILIPINO?

The Philippines continues to be one of the top sending counties in the world in terms of workforce and has about 1.6 million overseas Filipino workers (legally) around the globe. In 2014, the remittances from this group amounted to 26.92 billion US Dollars (USD) which contributed to as much as 8.5 percent of the Gross Domestic Product (GDP) (BSP, 2015), while the most recent figures for the year 2020 shows an increase in remittances of over

30 billion USD (BSP, n.d.). The quest to cross borders stems from job and financial opportunities perceived to be available in other countries that the national government is otherwise unable to provide. The income differentials between the sending and receiving countries also continue to be among the primary sources of this international migration. Given the sheer amount of exported labor and its contribution to the country's economy, the Philippine government established the Philippine Overseas Employment Administration (POEA) in 1982 to assist Filipino migrant workers. The POEA has the legal mandate to protect the rights of migrant workers. Among its functions include conducting a pre-deployment orientation seminar that advises those going overseas for the first time. The POEA also provides repatriation assistance and assists victims of illegal recruitment (POEA, 2015). With the need to further protect and ensure the welfare of the Filipino migrant workers and their families, the Migrant Workers and Overseas Filipinos Act was also enacted in 1995 (RA 8042, 1995).

The facility in the English language of the Filipinos—as a result of American education and pop culture bequeathed by its American colonizers shows how this linguistic capital has benefited the populace in its purpose to gain occupation overseas. This fluency has also translated to higher wages and better job chances for those joining the international labor market. Unfortunately, the contradictory and decline in social class mobility is evident for those entering the low-skilled market (e.g., domestic helpers), most of which would give up their middle-class status and higher education qualification in exchange for financial advancement opportunities that are otherwise lacking in the Philippines. It is not surprising then to hear of a teacher by profession in the Philippines migrating overseas to work as a domestic worker (Parrenas, 2001; Symaco, 2011). Preference for the Filipino domestic worker manifests in the West and South given their articulacy in the language, among other things.

> Those rich Italians with big villas by the coast, you will see that they employ Filipino domestic helpers, and they pay higher than what others on average would pay an Eastern European worker because the Filipinos *speak better English* and work harder than other nationalities.
>
> Filipino domestic workers [in Greece] are paid more [than other nationalities] because they are more educated and *speak better English*.
>
> We prefer hiring a Filipino [in Malaysia] and do not mind paying more because they are educated and *speak better English* than other Asians. (emphasis by the author)

Filipinos are also spread in other professions. For those in the service industry where facility in the English language is required, this gives them a competitive edge over other foreign workers. Lan (2003) notes this linguistic advantage posed by the Filipino workers in Taiwan, which have served as a "symbolic domination and resistance in their daily communications and job negotiation" (p. 133). The apparent play of linguistic advantage as expounded by Bourdieu's linguistic capital (1991), similar to other cultural capital, reflects the institutionalized power relations as predetermined by the "preferred" language as espoused by the market determining it. The preference, for instance, of the British English over other "forms of English was exhibited in England"'s (1996) study of foreign domestic workers in Toronto:

> Being British, the things we get away with! Our English accents—people just bend over backwards to help us, "Oh what lovely accent!, 'What can I do for you?" . . . . [Employers] like the English accent, they like the way we speak, they like our education, the way we speak to the children. (p. 209)

This preference is also asserted by Lan (2003, p. 151) where the economic distribution of capital means that well-educated employers are cautious of the Filipino domestic workers' ironically, "bad, substandard [and] unrefined" English as possibly affecting their children's English skills.

As reflective of the actual language practice and management in the country, the BPO market (mainly call centers) has shaped and re-introduced the strengthening of the English language policy and challenging the more recently institutionalized MTB-MLE agenda in the education setting, where more university graduates are lured to employment in the BPO industry (Symaco, 2011). Such is the expanse of the sector that it is predicted to create a structural shift in revenues where the BPO commerce is set to surpass the already significant foreign remittances from migrant workers (Curran Daly & Associates, 2019). As earlier discussed, this endogenous growth approach mirrors both the human capital dimension and ICT features of progress. But despite the acknowledgment of the country's articulacy in the English language as a factor for the BPO sector's expansion, issues are still raised regarding the unequal and sub-par training in the English language as exhibited by some call center applicants and as reflected above in the case of some migrant workers (Bernardo 2004; Frignal, 2007; Tupas, 2015).

The definition of English as the language of globalization and modernity well describes the situation above where an explicit language policy may not necessarily be translated to actual practice and management. The realization rings true in the actual practice of the MTB-MLE and also by Burton''s (2013) study, which revealed the preference of stakeholders (i.e., teachers and parents) in using the English language over the vernacular in the classroom teaching and the home environment. As anticipated in that study, the global command of English and its opportunities (e.g., more accessible entry to the labor market) defines the implicit language use of the community as challenging the top-down policy of the MTB-MLE. The study also shows the lack of community involvement in policy orientations. It highlights the lack of resources and teacher training, as similarly revealed by Spolsky (2004), as potential challenges faced by the mother-tongue-based education policy. While Tupas (2015), on the one hand, though contentious, polemically positions policies in education in the Philippines that may highlight the "internalized, certainly colonially induced, hatred toward the mother tongues." (p. 121).

CLOSING REMARKS

This chapter illustrates the discordance between language policy and actual language practice and use in the Philippines. The dominant role of the English language as the language for modernization speaks of the supposed better economic opportunities in line for individuals with fluency in the language. We have also seen likely implications in terms of the decline and possible elimination of minority languages in support of adhering to "one" global or national language. As in the case of the Philippines, where controversies still surround the choice of Filipino as the national language, all too linked as the predominant language of the center of power that is Manila. Given the high degree of linguistic heterogeneity in the country and a strong politics of clientelism, the misconstrued "neutrality" of the English language that may prevent the marginalization of other indigenous languages (i.e., over Filipino) is evident. The linguistic capital promoted by Bourdieu is unmistakable where Tollefson (1991) considers the English language as "the" language of education, which can only so often serve as a significant social stratifier. This feature dictates the outcome of opportunities for the Filipinos, depending on their access or otherwise, to elite institutions that provide the desired quality in English language training.

The preference to acquire "good" English also threatens the successful implementation of the mother-tongue-based education policy in the country. And despite the cash-strapped features of the Philippines and the recognized issues of MTB-MLE programs such as additional training and references that require substantial resource generation, the divergent views of stakeholders in language policy, practice, and use, prefigures the lack of community involvement in language policy formation. Granted the country's desire to better the prospects of its population for development through an improved education setting expected in the MTB-MLE, the attention to the intricacies found in the contextual background is crucial. When one constructs the matters of socioeconomic, cultural, and political needs with its populations' desire to forge with modernity and globalization, only then will language education policy be its most powerful.

Note

This chapter is a revised and updated version of Lorraine Symaco's "Education, language policy and language use in the Philippines." *Language Problems and Language Planning.* 41(4): 87-102, 2017, John Benjamins, DOI: 10.1075/lplp.41.1.05sym. https://benjamins.com/catalog/lplp.

Chapter 6

Education and Language: A Multi-ethnic Approach

INTRODUCTION

This chapter discusses the issues of inclusion, identity formation, and marginalized languages as pertinent to the Philippines. It provides an overview of the different ethnic groups and the various languages spoken in the Philippines, the current status of the local languages, and the historical background of Philippine education. The declaration of the national language led to the implementation and reforms of the education language policies, which resulted in the use of Filipino, English, and the mother tongue as the media of instructions (MOI). In particular, the role of the MTB-MLE policy, which aims to address such issues and the inherent complications faced by this policy in terms of teacher training, resources, and non-use of policy in certain settings, will be assessed.

ETHNICITY AND LANGUAGE EDUCATION IN THE PHILIPPINES

The Philippines is a multilingual and multicultural country that contributed to the country's linguistic and cultural diversity. The Summer Institute of Linguistics (SIL) survey shows that the Philippines has 181 languages or dialects (Dayag, 2016; Campesino and Telen, 2014; Lewis et al., 2013). This would mean that roughly the languages in the Philippines would range from 181 to 195. As discussed in the previous chapters, throughout the Philippines, there are eight major languages recognized to have a considerable number of native speakers, such as Tagalog, Ilocano, Bicol, Kapampangan, Pangasinense, Cebuano, Hiligaynon, and Waray. These eight languages are now taught in schools as the mother-tongue language, although many of these languages are not extensively studied yet (Gonzales, 2017).

The Filipino ethnic group is categorized into several ethnicities. The largest ethnic groups are scattered throughout the three big Islands of Luzon, Visayas, and Mindanao, that include the Tagalog, Cebuano, Ilocano, Bicolano, Kapampangan, Maranao, Maguindanao, and Tausug. There are also several aborigines throughout the country.

Due to the mixed ethnic origins of Filipinos as a product of intermarriages from one ethnic group to another and from one race to another, it is difficult to identify precisely the ethnic backgrounds of many Filipinos. There have been Filipinos who married people from Asia, Africa, America, Europe, and Oceania (Dumanig, 2010; Cabilao-Valencia, 2015). With the emergence of migration and globalization, the demographics of ethnic groups in the Philippines have changed in the past years.

The diverse ethnic groups reflect the various languages in the Philippines. Apart from the ethnic languages and the national language, many Filipinos speak English, a second language that has exponentially increased its number of speakers. Many Filipinos, if not all, are multilingual speakers who speak the local language, Filipino, English, and other Philippine languages (Dumanig et al., 2020). The multilingual nature of Filipinos is reflected in its country's language policy.

Languages and ethnicity in the Philippines always co-exist. According to Kentjono (1986, p. 1), "the Philippines has 110 ethnolinguistic groups, and they comprise almost 15% of the Philippine population." All these ethnic groups are given support from the government as stated in the Indigenous People's Rights Act (or IPRA) in 1997, recognizing the indigenous peoples' inherent rights, including their right to self-governance and self-determination; rights to ancestral domains, and the requirement of free, prior informed consent on any development on their ancestral domains or those that have a specific impact on them (Penaranda, 2019, p. 1). These various ethnolinguistic groups make the Philippines a unique position in Southeast Asia to show the world how diversity and unity come together as one unified country.

Many ethnic groups are identified through the language that they speak. For example, the Cebuanos speak the Cebuano language, the Surigaonons speak the Surigaonon language, the Tagalog speak the Tagalog language, and the Ilongos speak the Ilongo language. Both language and ethnicity may equate to culture, and they could be a source of unifying and dividing people.

The Philippines always aims to unify the multicultural and multilingual Filipinos and to enhance nation-building. Such objectives resulted in declaring the national language and creating the education language policy. According to Kentjono (1986, p. 294), "to own a national language entails the love for the national language. . . . Cultivation of our national language . . .

is moreover a part of our nation-building." Declaring the national language is not enough to develop and enhance the Filipino identity; it is also necessary to include other ethnic languages as part of the Filipino identity. It must be noted that language is synonymous with culture, where language reflects the culture and vice versa (Kuo and Lai, 2006). This means that having an inclusive society will further enhance the Filipino identity as one country and one people.

The country's education language policy gives importance to unifying the people and, at the same time, developing a Filipino identity. After the Philippines gained independence from the USA and declared Filipino as the national language, the education language policy underwent some changes and development to meet the needs of the Filipino people and the needs of the students. After several studies and reforms, in 1974, the Bilingual Education Policy (BEP) was implemented. The policy aims to make the Filipinos bilingual by achieving competence in Filipino and English and use both languages as the media of instruction at all levels. The local languages function as auxiliary languages, particularly in grade 1 and grade 2 (Tupas and Lorente, 2014).

The BEP's aim to enhance competence in English and Filipino could be considered a success. For several years after implementing the language policy, many Filipinos have been able to speak the national language and English fluently (Axel, 2011). It shows that Filipino, as the national language, is spoken by approximately 69 million and 24 million Filipinos who speak Tagalog as a native language (Eberhard et al., 2020). Both languages served as lingua franca for intranational and international communication. Smolicz (1984) mentioned that the Philippines needs a national language that would function as a "lingua franca" for all Filipinos. BEP seemed to focus on Filipino and English, and minimal attention was given to the ethnic languages. The BEP has been successful in promoting Filipino as the national language and English as a second language.

In 2009, a new language policy, the Mother-Tongue-Based Multilingual Education (MTB-MLE), was formulated and implemented in 2012. The policy stated that the MTB-MLE should be implemented in all public schools, specifically in Kindergarten, grades 1, 2, and 3. Some local languages in the Philippines are currently used in teaching grades 1 to 3, while English and Filipino are introduced starting grade 4 (Burton, 2013). There are 19 recognized regional languages in the Philippines as ordered and permitted by the Department of Education under the Mother-Tongue-Based Education (MTB-MLE) (Gatil, 2021). Such approved languages are used as MOI in schools in different regions of the country (Burton, 2013).

CURRENT STATUS OF THE LOCAL LANGUAGES IN THE PHILIPPINES

Language diversity in the Philippines prompts the government to give importance to the national language, official languages, and the minority languages spoken in various provinces of the country. The implementation of the mother-tongue-based multilingual education serves as a tool that helps the minority languages be recognized, intellectualized, and raise their social functions.

Of the many languages in the Philippines, only 19 local languages were selected to be taught in the MTB-MLE program. This means that more than a hundred local languages are not taught as the mother tongue. According to Trudell (2016), the plurality of languages in society may pose many challenges and repercussions of choosing a mother tongue as the medium of instruction (MOI) from among many alternatives, which may result in a mismatch between the mother tongue as medium of instruction and the students' first languages. For example, in the provinces of Surigao del Norte and Surigao del Sur, there are varieties of Surigaonon language such as Surigaonon (commonly spoken in some towns in the province of Surigao del Norte), Tandaganon, and Cantilanon (commonly spoken in the province of Surigao del Sur). Choosing Surigaonon as the mother-tongue language that will be taught may not apply to some places in the province of Surigao del Norte and Surigao del Sur. Such an issue poses some problems to the teachers on how the mother tongue be taught to students who speak different varieties of Surigaonon language. It also brings more confusion to the parents who speak different varieties of mother tongue. It seems that the status of the mother-tongue languages was overlooked by the policymakers when implementing the language policy. This is also a result of minimal to no research conducted about the mother-tongue languages in the country before the implementation of the MTB-MLE (Merriam, 1988).

The limited sources of many local languages reflect the number of understudied languages. This means that many mother-tongue languages are not studied and fully intellectualized yet. The implementation of the MTB-MLE could have been effective if most of the languages were studied and already have standardized orthography, grammar, and phonology. The challenges that most teachers encounter in teaching the mother tongue are the limited resources of the language/s they teach.

In order to make the language policy more inclusive, ready, and prepared to be taught to the young learners, extensive research must be done first to all mother tongue or local languages and eventually standardize them. Doing this will also prevent any mother-tongue languages from becoming extinct or eventually die. The Philippines has four ethnic languages that are classified as extinct and have only a few speakers (Lewis and Simons, 2015). In a study conducted by Headland (2003), he found thirty Negrito languages are considered endangered or dying in the Philippines. A language is classified as endangered when it is faced with the imminent danger of dying out (Cahill, 1999). With the increasing popularity and importance of globalization, migration, and the internet, there is a high chance that ethnic or minority languages will eventually become extinct or die out when they are not maintained and intellectualized. The ethnic languages in the Philippines are no exemption to this. The MTB-MLE is an acceptable policy that will help revitalize the mother-tongue languages, but more works are needed to succeed.

MTB-MLE AND TEACHERS' TRAINING AND PREPAREDNESS

The introduction of MTB-MLE in the Philippine education system is a reflection of the multi-ethnic and multilingual nature of the country. With the decreasing number of younger Filipinos who speak their mother tongue or ethnic languages, the MTB-MLE could be the possible solution to allow learners to learn the ethnic languages in the Philippines.

The challenges in implementing MTB-MLE in primary school are the teachers' fluency in listening, reading, speaking, and writing of the mother-tongue language. Some school-teachers do not have the fluency of some mother-tongue languages because of their variations (Alidou, 2003). For example, as mentioned earlier, in the provinces of Surigao del Norte and Surigao del Sur where the Surigaonon language is used and recognized as the mother tongue. However, the Surigaonon language has variations, such as the Surigaonon, also known as "Jaun-Jaun or Waya-Waya," and the Tandaganon, also known as "Tinandag, Naturalis or Tagon-on" (Dumanig, 2015). Teachers who speak Tandaganon might not be proficient in another variation of the Jaun-Jaun or Waya-Waya Surigaonon or vice versa. Having no standardized mother-tongue language may confuse the teachers as to which specific variety must be taught in a mother tongue classroom. In a scenario like this, teachers need proper training on how this situation be handled inside the classroom.

Another factor that needs to be considered in MTB-MLE implementation is that some teachers who come from different provinces do not speak the same mother tongue as the students. To prepare the teachers to teach the learners' mother tongue, necessary training must be done; otherwise, it would be very challenging for the teacher to teach the language that they are not proficient. Alidou and Brock-Utne (2006, p. 85) argued that "the use of unfamiliar languages forces teachers to use traditional and teacher-centered teaching methods." The teachers' lack of linguistic knowledge of the medium of instruction may pose several serious issues in teaching and learning. To make the mother-tongue education more effective, teachers must have the fluency of the language in both oral and written forms. Studies show that "there are several bilingual teachers who face serious professional challenges because they may be able to speak the language of instruction but with limited skills in reading and writing in that language" (Alidou, 2003, p. 114).

Malone and Malone (2011) suggested some basic content of teacher training for MTB-MLE that includes the trainee's language development; MTB-MLE students' background knowledge, and skills; learning theories, and good practices relating to L1 development; theories, and good practices relating to second language acquisition; theories and good practices relating to using L1 and L2 as languages of instruction, curriculum; and instructional materials, and teaching principles for MTB MLE. Providing teachers with sufficient training will eventually help them succeed in the implementation of mother-tongue-based education.

MTB-MLE AND TEACHING MATERIALS

The other challenge is the availability of instructional materials in 19 local languages (Eberhard et al., 2020). Studies have shown that limited teaching materials impacted the quality of teaching the mother tongue in some provinces in the Philippines. Instructional materials needed to teach the mother tongue are not readily available in most local languages (Wa-Mbaleka, 2014). Rubi and Molina (2020) argued that one of the significant drawbacks of the MTB-MLE program is the lack of instructional materials that augment the learning process in the classroom. Rosario et al., (2016) highlighted the issues in listening where teachers do not have the available audio recording for their listening activities. Rost (1994, pp. 141–42) argued that "listening is vital in the language classroom because it provides input for the learner." This is crucial because if there is no comprehensible input, language learning will not take place. Krashen (2003) emphasized that we acquire language and develop literacy when we understand messages; that is when we understand what we hear and what we read. In a study conducted by Rosario et al. (2016, p. 3), they interviewed some teachers, and they mentioned that:

> We don't have an audio recording for Hiligaynon, unlike in the English and Filipino subjects. We are still hoping that the Department of Education will provide us audio recordings so that it will add more interest to the students to listen. Most of the time, they cannot comprehend when they listen to profound Hiligaynon words. They tend not to listen because they find it boring" and "We

just focus on the books provided by the Department of Education which is limited. Thus, the vocabulary that the students learned is also limited.

There are also very limited books in the mother-tongue languages. Many of the languages do not have any books or even dictionaries, and the teachers rely only on whatever information they get from the internet or other sources (Espada et al., 2017; Lartec et al., 2014; Namanya, 2017; Rivera, 2017; Rosario et al., 2016). There were no textbooks available for teachers and students. It is important to note that textbooks are essential in language teaching; they guide the teachers in creating the syllabus, teaching approaches and methodologies, and the materials to be used (Zohrabi et al., 2012). Textbooks are also useful instruments that provide the learners with the means to learn on their own, and they also help learners to plan and organize their learning (Cunningsworth, 1995).

Alberto et al. (2016) further emphasized the issues and challenges in teaching the mother-tongue-based multilingual education in grades 1 and 2 that the scarcity of instructional materials hinders the enhancement of the reading, listening, speaking, and writing skills of learners. Although teachers could create their own reading and writing materials, some mother-tongue languages in the Philippines do not have standardized grammar and orthography. Implementing a policy with minimal or no available resources will make teaching the mother tongue less successful. Despite such shortcomings, MTB-MLE is helpful in other aspects because it allows the learners to explain their ideas and thoughts in their first language, and it also facilitates learning English or other languages (Alberto et al., 2016).

In some places, some textbooks used in teaching the mother-tongue language were haphazardly made. Some teachers published their own books with no extensive research, reviews, and editing (Eslit, 2017). These self-published books and textbooks in mother-tongue languages may pose significant problems in language teaching and learning. This is one of the loopholes of the Philippine Government for not considering the availability of the teaching materials before implementing the policy. Due to limited textbooks, books, and other teaching materials, teachers are not able to deliver the appropriate content and teaching methods (Lartec et al., 2014; Rosario et al., 2016;).

MTB-MLE AND SPEAKERS' ATTITUDE TOWARD LOCAL LANGUAGE

Language attitude refers to any affective, cognitive, or behavioral index of evaluative reactions toward different language varieties or speakers (Ryan and Giles, 1982, p. 7). It can predict the speakers' behavior toward a language, their language choice, and language loyalty (Obiols, 2002). This means that the teaching of the mother tongue should not focus only on developing the language proficiency of the learners, but it is also important to inculcate a positive attitude to the mother tongue that the learners speak.

Language attitude can be explained based on the behaviorist and mentalist perspectives. Behaviorists believe that human actions can be determined through individual responses based on the specific context (Somblingo and Alieto, 2019). The behaviorist's perspective argues that an attitude is a behavioral unit that can be exhibited through the speaker's responses (Perloff, 2003). This view has been supported by Allport, as cited in Papuc (2016, 1), who defined language attitude as "a learned disposition to think, feel, and behave towards a person in a particular way." Such disposition is either an indication of the speaker's personal or social characteristics. This means that a person's attitude toward a language or other languages is not inherent; however, it can be argued that attitude is learned and mastered, resulting in a favorable or unfavorable attitude (Papuc, 2016).

On the other hand, language attitude is also viewed differently by mentalists. They believe that attitude is an internal state and could not be directly observed outwardly. Baker (1992) argues that the speaker's attitude cannot be predicted by outward behavior because people have the ability to conceal their inner attitudes. What is seen externally does not reflect the internal attitude of a person. Research shows that there is evidence that supports the idea that attitude exists in the mind of a person and could sometimes be hardly identified or determined directly through external behavior (McKenzie, 2010). Both the behaviorist and Mentalist perspectives explain how language attitudes are learned, developed, and expressed.

In the Philippines, people's language attitude toward the mother tongue and English may vary depending on their language orientation. Still, generally, most people have a positive attitude toward English because it is viewed to be more beneficial (Tupas, 2015), and it alleviates the socioeconomic status of the Filipinos (Javier and Vicerra, 2010; Rafael and Rosario, 2011). Somblingo and Alieto (2019) found in their study that Filipino students exhibit a "very positive" attitude toward English as compared to the local languages. These findings are further supported by Gallego and Zubiri (2011), who argued that in Pangasinan province, parents prefer that their children be taught in Filipino and English than in the mother-tongue language.

On the contrary, the language attitude toward the mother tongue is not desirable (Esteron, 2020) and may pose challenges in achieving success in the MTB-MLE program. Ellis (1997) argues that negative language attitudes have an impact on language learning success. In fact, one of the major problems in achieving the long-term success of the MTB-MLE is the attitude of the speakers of the local languages. Many people have the impression that the mother tongue is not desirable compared to Filipino and English (Esteron, 2020). Such a negative impression has been passed from one generation to the next, which is one reason why learners have less motivation to learn the vernacular language. Consequently, many people in the Philippines value the national language and English more because of their economic and social benefits (Dumanig et al., 2020). Although Filipino is preferred over the vernacular, some students also believe that learning and speaking Filipino can also be a barrier in English language learning (Esteron, 2020).

In general, people highly favor English compared to many languages because it is packaged as the language of opportunities (Mahboob and Cruz, 2013). Other than that, the status of English as an international and global language has also increased people's inclination to learn and speak the language. Studies show that the English language in Southeast Asia plays a major role in people's employability (Zainuddin et al., 2019). Due to the economic benefits that people get from English, they tend to value it compared to other languages.

In the Philippines, the increasing importance of the national language and English may result in people's decreasing interest in learning the local languages. The declining interest will eventually influence people's attitudes toward the language. The negative attitude toward the vernacular language will slowly lessen the interest to maintain the language and may shift to the majority language. Language shift refers to the gradual displacement, usually of a minority language in favor of the dominant language by community members (Hornberger, 2010). Displacing the minority language may also displace people's identity. The implementation of MTB-MLE in the Philippines is not just to enhance the ability to speak the local language but also to enhance the ethnic identity of the speakers through the local language. A study conducted by Bautista and Gonzalez (1986) on language and ethnicity in the Philippines emphasizes that the mother tongue directly impacts the ethnic identity construction among Filipinos. Chapter 3 discusses the self-categorization theory, which highlights that identity is constructed through language use.

Therefore, to make MTB-MLE a success, this requires collaborative work between schools and the community. Learning the mother tongue in school can be supported by the community so that the learners can appreciate the functions of the mother tongue outside the school. If younger generations see that the school and the community provide importance to the mother tongue, then interests in learning the language will be developed. Consequently, it may influence a more positive linguistic behavior of the minority language speakers. Giles et al. (1987, as cited in Civico, 2019) explained language vitality and categorized the factors that affect language vitality into three categories such as the status factors, demographic factors, and institutional support factors. The "status factors include variables such as the socio-economic conditions of speakers, the perception of the language in terms of prestige (or lack thereof), and the sociohistorical weight of the language; the demographic factors include variables such as the absolute number of speakers and rates of emigration and immigration; and the institutional support factors, include the formal and informal support to the language provided by various institutions, such as legal recognition and language education programs" (Giles et al., 1987 as cited in Civico, 2019, p. 4).

The implementation of MTB-MLE in the Philippines could have been a significant contribution to enhance the ethnic identity of the younger generations by learning the mother tongue. However, implementing the new education language policy has not anticipated the issues on the teachers' materials and training in delivering the mother-tongue classes.

After a few years of implementing the MTB-MLE, many studies were conducted to measure the effectiveness and success of the language policy. Issues related to teachers' training and preparation to teach the course and the lack of available materials to teach the mother tongue resulted in some unfavorable responses to the MTB-MLE. Wa-Mbaleka (2014) conducted a study of 476 Filipino teachers of English of their perceptions about the implementation of MTB-MLE, and the result showed a negative perception among English teachers. Such responses indicate that MTB-MLE still needs more improvement to make it more effective. On the other hand, when the non-teaching professionals were surveyed of their perceptions of the MTB-MLE program, similar findings were revealed and highlighted that the teaching of the mother tongue robbed the children of learning English (Mahboob and Cruz, 2013). The responses from both teaching and non-teaching professionals are consistent and may reflect that MTB-MLE has not become fully successful yet after its few years of implementation. What lies ahead of this policy can be an uphill battle against an ingrained hierarchization of language (Belvis and Morauda-Gutierrez, 2019). Currently, the use of the mother tongue at the primary level does not guarantee that learners will eventually give equal importance to the ethnic languages, national language, and English. In fact, Nolasco (2013) argued that MTB-MLE is only officially recognized on paper, but the actual practice in the classroom is still predominantly bilingual.

FUTURE DIRECTIONS OF MTB-MLE

The current situation of MTB-MLE in the Philippines is moving toward a favorable direction based on the 2015 national performance per mother tongue among grade 3 students in 19 mother tongue languages. The mean percentage scores of grade 3 students in 19 mother-tongue languages range from 54 to 85 (Ocampo, 2017). The results serve as indicators that the implementation of mother-tongue education has a reasonable rate of success. Espada (2012) argued that it brings more success in learning when teachers and students share the same languages. This means that using the mother tongue as the medium of instruction in school facilitates a better learning experience (Dressler and Kamil 2008; Geva and Genesee 2008). Studies have shown that MTB-MLE is successful, particularly in countries with few mother-tongue languages (Kang, 2012).

The current MTB-MLE policy in the country has shown progress regarding mother-tongue education (Monje et al., 2019). However, as discussed in Chapter 6, many issues from the teachers' training, policy implementation, and availability of the teaching materials remain challenging to many educators have impacted the overall results of the policy implementation.

The emergence of the COVID-19 as a global pandemic has contributed to the challenging situations in implementing the MTB-MLE. However, it has also benefited young learners because online classes have allowed learners to stay at home. Parents or other family members are able to assist the children in their learning using the mother tongue since most parents do not speak English at home (Tecson, 2020). In some ways, online education has allowed the members of the family to assist the learners in their learning using the mother tongue as the medium of communication.

In the coming years, it is expected that more training for teachers and mother-tongue materials need to be developed to improve the MTB-MLE further. This means that this policy will continue in the next coming years despite the criticism from other scholars and educators.

Chapter 7

Closing Remarks: Education and Language in the Philippines

INTRODUCTION

We have examined the roles of education and language in the Philippines, where various dynamics come into play—from the features of modernization—linking the commodification and standardization of education associated with globalization tendencies and the use of a :common" language in line with development goals and sociocultural and political indices. In the sections to follow, we sum up the overarching narrative of this book and present readers with the importance of a contextualized language-in-education policies as relevant to the Philippines.

LANGUAGE EDUCATION POLICY AND IDENTITY FORMATION

The language plurality in the Philippines and its colonial past contribute to the identity formation of the Filipinos. The Philippines is one of the countries in Southeast Asia that has 181 languages (Campesino and Telen, 2014; Dayag, 2016; Lewis et al., 2013), excluding the dialects. The many islands of the country are grouped into three major islands, Luzon, Visayas, and Mindanao, and further grouped into different regions. Almost every region of the country has different languages and ethnic groups. Out of 181 languages in 18 regions of the country, there are fourteen major languages aside from the national language. Of the fourteen languages, four languages have approximately nine million or more speakers, such as Tagalog, Cebuano, Ilocano, and Hiligaynon (Eberhard et al., 2020). On the other hand, ten languages such as Waray, Bikol, Kapampangan, Pangasinan, Maranao, Tausug, Maguindanao, Chavacano, Karay-a, and Surigaonon have one million to three million speakers (Eberhard et al., 2020). The various ethnic groups and ethnic languages have brought complexity in planning and mandating the education language policy.

The historical development of language education in the Philippines reflects the linguistic and cultural diversity of the country. There are many languages in the Philippines that are not yet intellectualized, and through the language education policy, some Philippine languages have been intellectualized. When one language is intellectualized, expanded its functions, and raised its status in a multilingual society, other languages may eventually become minority languages. This results in language inequality, and peoples' attitudes toward the majority and minority languages may change. Studies show that minority language groups tend to lose their language over the course of a few generations (Fishman, 1972; Glenn and DeJong, 1996; Veltman, 1983). Eventually, those languages that have limited functions may become extinct and eventually die. Therefore, language planning can help multilingual countries to preserve all languages, particularly the minority languages. Due to language plurality and colonization in the Philippines, language planning and language policy become more complex.

When the Philippines was colonized by Spain in the sixteenth century for 350 years, the Spanish language was added to the languages spoken in the country (Lacsamana, 1990). In the early part of the twentieth century, 60 percent of Filipinos spoke Spanish as a second language (Weedon, 2019). Despite the limited number of Filipinos who speak Spanish, it has significantly influenced some languages in the Philippines. Studies show that a third of the Filipino language is derived from Spanish words, constituting some 4,000 loan words (Weedon, 2019). There is 0.5 percent of Filipinos who can speak Spanish, but still, the Philippines is considered as the country in Asia that has the most number of Spanish speakers (Weedon, 2019). This book discusses some Philippine languages influenced by Spanish, and they are evident in naming the months, numbers, streets, names of people, names of places, and names of celebrations.

The Spanish introduced formal education to Filipinos but this was limited only to the elite who could afford to study. Spanish was used as the medium of instruction (MOI) by default in all schools (Bernabe, 1987). The establishment of schools, colleges, and universities paved the way for Filipinos to be educated, and many of those who studied eventually became proficient in Spanish (Bernabe, 1987). Since the Spanish language was used as MOI, the education during that time did not contribute to the development of the Philippine languages and culture; however, educated Filipinos learned more about the imposed Spanish language and culture. Because only a few Filipinos could afford to go to schools, by the end of the Spanish regime, only 2.46 percent of the adult Filipinos could speak Spanish (Gonzalez, 1980).

Generally, for 300 years under Spanish rule, Filipinos were deprived of developing their own local languages and culture.

During the American occupation, English replaced Spanish as the MOI in all schools. Such a form of linguistic imperialism elevated the status of the colonizers' language and marginalized the local languages. It somehow impacted how Filipinos regarded their local languages. The colonizers' language eventually became the language of the elite, while the local languages were considered subordinate (Reyes, 2017).

Identity is always tied up with the language; it can be said that the Filipino identity for four hundred years was not cultivated and downplayed by the colonizers who created and imposed an identity toward the Filipinos as second-class citizens in their own country (Mateo, 2016). Such forced identity formation may lead to a negative attitude toward the Filipino language and culture.

When the Philippines gained its independence from the Americans, the Filipinos gained their freedom and provided opportunities to develop and promote their own language, culture, and identity. The independence brought to the declaration of Filipino as the national language, and Filipino and English as official languages. The Filipino language was declared to unify the Filipinos and to create a Filipino identity reflected in its national language (Axel, 2011).

Many years after the Philippines gained independence, the country implemented the Bilingual Education Policy (BEP) in 1974. This bilingual policy, which was revised in 1987, stated that English and Filipino are the languages of education and the country's official languages. BEP was successful in making Filipinos bilingual in English and Filipino, but the importance of learning English was favored more than that of the national language. The preference for English was influenced by the international status of English and the economic mobility that it brings to people who can speak the language proficiently. This resulted in a mismatch between the education language policy with the actual classroom practice. Although it is clear in the BEP that both Filipino and English are the MOI at all levels (Bernabe, 1987).

However, emphasis on English and Filipino further diminishes the functions of the ethnic languages even in the community. The young generations started to see the lesser value of their ethnic languages and eventually impacted their interest in using the ethnic language even in the home domain. One of the reasons for language loss, which results in identity loss, is the presence of dominant languages in a multilingual society (Dastgoshadeh and Jalilzadeh, 2011).

Despite the popularity of English, studies show that the English language proficiency of the graduates slowly declined (Torres, 2009; Bawa, 2020). According to the 2020 report released by the international education company Education First (EF), the Philippines ranked 27 in the English Proficiency

Index, lower than the previous ranking (Calvelo, 2020). This means that students are losing their ethnic language and English language proficiency. Another study shows that based on the teachers' reports, they believe that many students in the Philippines lack English language proficiency (Bawa, 2020). The declining proficiency in the English language has triggered the creation of a new language education policy aimed to broadly enhance the English language, ethnic languages, national language, and Filipino identity.

Introducing the Filipino and English languages as mediums of instruction may not be sufficient to enhance the Filipino identity. To fully understand and inculcate Filipino identity into the minds of Filipino learners, there is a need to include ethnic languages in the education system. It must be noted that language symbolizes and signals the speaker's identity (Rovira, 2008). This is one of the reasons why the Mother-Tongue-Based Multilingual Education (MTB-MLE) was implemented to replace the BEP.

The MTB-MLE aims to enhance the local language proficiency and to develop the local identity formation that leads to the construction of Filipino identity. Walter and Dekker (2011) argued that multilingual students who gained literacy in their first language obtained higher academic achievement than students who learned in a second or third language. Moreover, when the learners' first language is established at an earlier age, acquiring the second language proficiency is easier (Hu, 2016). The education language policy of the country was not only implemented to develop the language proficiency of the Filipinos in their mother tongue, the national language, and English but also to enhance the Filipino identity. Studies show that MTB-MLE also allows the effective use of more than two languages for literacy and instruction (Department of Education, 2016).

In the MTB-MLE, the mother-tongue languages are used as the medium of instruction from Kindergarten to grade 3, while Filipino and English are used from grade 4 onward. The teaching of the mother tongue aims to develop the language proficiency of the students' first language and enhance their local identity. Studies also show that in any educational contexts that do not give importance to the mother tongues, will result in an education having lesser relevance to the students (MacKenzie, 2009). On the contrary, MTB-MLE also poses several issues, particularly on the preparedness of the teachers who teach the language and the availability of the teaching materials. Teachers are challenged by a dearth of supplementary references, and teachers themselves find ways to obtain resources to teach the mother tongue (Williams et al., 2014).

When the MTB-MLE was implemented, the notion about national identity was evident as Clots-Figueras and Masella (2013) argued that educational policy might impact identity formation. "Language is always linked with identity, and in order to save, preserve, and promote identity, speakers must attempt to save the language" (Dastgoshadeh and Jalilzadeh, 2011, p. 659). The MTB-MLE focuses on the formation of the Filipino national identity through language use. Exposing children to the mother tongue and the national language during their formative years and allowing them to understand who they and their ethnic roots are, will eventually enhance their sense of belonging to a particular group or community (Bang, 2015). Apart from being able to speak the ethnic language or the mother tongue and the national language proficiently, young learners are able to understand the group or social category where he or she belongs (Stets and Burke, 2000). Gumperz (1982) argued that language creates the speaker's identity and identifies their social group membership. Through self-categorization, learners are able to categorize themselves as group members and eventually act similarly with other members with a common identity, group orientation, and behavior (Turner, 1991, p. 155; Turner and Onorato, 1999).

Apart from the mother tongue and the national language, the English language has also been used as the medium of instruction in the Philippine educational system. The English language that was viewed before as a language of the colonizer became the language of the Filipinos. A variety of Philippine English emerged as a distinct variety of the English language. Philippine English is not only used as a language for business, education, and international communication, but it also serves as a national identity marker for Filipinos. Filipinos are easily identified as other English speakers because of their lexical choices, pronunciation, and discourse style. Identifying themselves as Filipinos through their use of Philippine English enhances their group behavior because of the commonality of their self-concept (Mummendey and Otten, 2001; Turner, 1991; Turner and Onorato, 1999).

The implementation of the educational language policies in the Philippines: the BEP and MTB-MLE made a significant contribution in developing proficiency in the national language, English language, and the mother tongue. In addition, through language education, the ethnic and national identity of the Filipinos are further enhanced. As Baez (2002, p. 125) stated, "culture, identity, and language may be inextricable from each other; all create identity, or, at least, important aspects of identity. But language not only creates the contours of identity, but it also may set up the conditions for other kinds of inclusion and exclusion, belonging and not belonging, success and failure. . . ."

As discussed in this book, English language education in the Philippines will continue to improve the language policy and language instructions. The development and changes of the language policy will also have an impact on English language education in the recently implemented K to 12 curricula. This curriculum replaces the 10-year basic education to 12 years. Such additional years and improved curricula are supposed to provide ample time for students to master the concepts and skills and to prepare them for tertiary education (Rogayan and Villanueva, 2019; Trance and Trance, 2019).

EDUCATION, LANGUAGE, AND MODERNITY

In this book, we have also discussed the interrelated roles of education and language as it relates to broader development policies, highlighting the influence of language in education, with the latter seen as a crucial step for socioeconomic advancement. The focus on the need to "educate" one's population equipped with the skills needed for the knowledge economy draws back to the human capital approach earlier discussed. Despite critics pointing to the one-dimensional normative system of this theory (Bowles and Gintis, 1975), the mass expansion of education over the years validates its importance in governments' development policies. Linking this to modernization tendencies, where acquiring the "proper" education would result in better socioeconomic mobilities among populations, we see how despite the national allocation of governments to education, its simultaneous opening to market forces (especially in higher education) draws its questioning feature either as being nationalized or "marketized." Such features represent debates on the need for state intervention or-a neoliberal, free-market approaches deemed incompatible (Middleton, 2000).

With the continued rise and influence of markets in education, the need to "standardize" is seen in a two-pronged approach, through increased regulation of the sector as relevant, for instance, in trading, and the necessity of a common and standard language in delivering such service (Fairclough, 1989). As we have discussed, the former has seen interventions by the World Trade Organisation (WTO) through the General Agreement on Trade in Services (GATS). In addition, the increase in trans-national campuses and mobility in both students and academic staff mirrors this heightening global service. Parallel to this is the regionalization of education services as manifests, such as the ASEAN initiatives in the Mutual Recognition Arrangement (MRA) and the ASEAN University Network, and a desire for standardization of services through the ASEAN Qualifications Reference Framework (AQRF). Despite lacking a more robust framework than the European Union, such initiatives in the region speak of the reinforced role of the education sector in regional integration and development (Symaco and Tee, 2019).

The tread toward a more compact and integrated ASEAN through the ASEAN Economic Community (AEC) is expected to amplify education functions in socioeconomic advancement further. The continued globalization of services pushes for such standardizations and regionalization of education, likening it to the commodification of the sector (Scherrer, 2005).

These augments in regionalization are synonymous with the New Growth Theory empirics earlier defined, where novel and contemporary advances such as that in ICT help maintain the so-called "institutional thickness" and provide better access to education provisions (Amin and Thrift, 1995). But despite this advance, the reductionist bias of education access is continued through the increasing digital divide, ironically brought forward by supposed improvements to access by the service itself. Recent happenings worldwide, such as the global pandemic COVID19, exhibited the weaknesses of educational institutions through the inability to gain access to ICT services, where 50 perent of learners (826 million) worldwide do not have access to a household computer, and 46 percent (706 million) do not have household internet. The case is direr in developing countries wherein only one (1) teacher for every 56 students in primary education is trained in basic education and ICT services (UNESCO Institute of Statistics, 2020).

In the Philippines, access to education provision during this health emergency also mirrors the economic burdens through the closure of private education institutions (due to lack of enrollments). There were 3 million fewer students enrolled during the health emergency, and the decision of families to cross-enroll their children in government-funded public schools versus previous private school enrolments exemplifies this (Magsambol, 2020). Despite this, the advantages of ICT in employment opportunities in the Philippines are acknowledged with the contribution of the IT-BPO sector. This market sector is poised to generate 38.9 billion US Dollars (USD) by the year 2022, possibly taking over the contributions of Overseas Filipino Workers (OFW) remittances (Curran Daly & Associates, 2019). This harnessed workforce and employment opportunity in the country stems from cheaper labor options and the proficiency of the Filipinos with the English language. This skill also illustrates the advantages for the Filipinos working overseas, where their knowledge of the English language allows for greater mobility and higher wages prospects. Notwithstanding criticisms to the fluency of English among the Filipinos (Symaco, 2011), compared to other Asia-Pacific Economic Cooperation (APEC) countries, the Philippines has a "relatively more opportunity to export its human resources to countries requiring English communication in skilled labor and domestic help" (Friginal 2007, p. 333). The intercultural ability of the Filipinos to transcend communications in the language is also noted:

> (T)he goal of English as an International Language (EIL), i.e., "international intelligibility," seems to have been achieved by Filipinos in communicating with both native and non-native speakers of English in many settings . . . the quality of English spoken and used in the Philippines could stand on its own and

be considered a self-determining variety of English which is deployed across structures equipped to fully function in international settings. (ibid, pp. 333–34)

The qualifications standardization desired in the ASEAN also emulates this through language use. As discussed in previous chapters, the role of English in the region echoes the global reach of the language, all too often equated with modernity and development.

> One of the primary consequences of English's global spread is that it now operates as the pre-eminent medium of international communication in the modern world. It is used as a lingua franca by various transnational political and economic associations while also serving as a medium of global communication in science, technology, business, and academics (Seargeant and Erling 2013, p. 2).

As aforementioned, country cases of differing English language policies related to its global presence are seen through bilingual policies in education and the need to equip students of their English language proficiencies (see Kirkpatrick, 2012). The link of language to international development has gained traction over the years. With English viewed as the language of opportunity (Wrigley et al., 2003), we see several studies that have investigated the part of English language in development (we must be mindful to not reduce development here as simply in economic aspects, but a broader cover that also ensures social improvements). Seargeant and Erling (2013) point to this emergent field of language and development where studies are categorized accordingly as (i) examining the relationships between language skills and economic gains (e.g., Martin and Lomperis, 2002; Grin, 1996); (ii) the exploration of ways in which language, education, and development may be linked (e.g., Rassool, 2007; Watson, 2012; Symaco, 2017); and (iii) investigations of how English language programs may be successful in meeting their objectives (and as they related to political and cultural issues) (Young, Sachdev, and Seedhouse, 2009; Brock-Utne, 2000, p. 4).

In the Philippines, the focus given to the English language is prominent, despite assertions of the need to engage learners with indigenous languages for better learning in schools. Given the status of English as the language of opportunity, the ability to master the language is prioritized where "even in rural areas, the use of English in schools is regarded as ideal and is not considered to be detrimental to overall learning" (Friginal 2007, p. 333). However, one should also note the disjoint in language policies and use in the country. Despite assertions to further the national or indigenous languages, English preference over these is known. It is also not unlikely to find members of the country's elite to be less than proficient in the national language than English. And while access to schooling may improve fluency in the English language and thus result in better employment prospects, success in further studies and training is still predisposed mainly to certain preconditions (e.g., socioeconomic backgrounds), which can maintain such disparities in the first place. This reality does not ring truer than in the developing Philippines. Those with means can access often better and more expensive schools while the majority face the lack of resources often defining public education institutions.

The prominent role of language in education in the country, as exemplified through the bilingual policy set in 1974, to the introduction of the mother-tongue-based multilingual education (MTB-MLE) in 2009 also shows the sociopolitical dynamics of language policy. The complex and intricate function of language stems from the desire to improve teaching and learning to the unavoidable center-periphery notion of language choice and use as linked to opportunities. Despite the best intentions to pivot language policies to improve teaching and learning better, contentions regarding the switch of media of instruction (e.g., bilingual policy to MTB-MLE) are ever-present. It was found that less than 10 percent of the schools surveyed for the MTB-MLE project did the implementation requirements for the program. At the same time, lack of both training and resources hampered its successful implementation (Oridnario, 2019). Despite such challenges, the push for perceived inclusion and pedagogical improvements are often unwittingly linked to language-in-education policies, while a more nuanced contextual investigation of the teaching and learning environment is often missed.

SOCIOCULTURAL DIMENSIONS OF EDUCATION AND LANGUAGE

We have generally discussed the role of culture and identity formation, among others, in education and language. Linking such features to pedagogy and access (social reproduction), we see how the multifaceted and nuanced relationship of education and language interplay. This social significance of language is not new when Emile Durkheim viewed this as a "social thing in the highest degree" in terms of civil-society building (Tada 2020, p. 597). The role of language in culture and society is manifest where late modernist concepts "on the historical and subjective nature of culture, conceived as co-constructed membership in a discourse community that shares a common social space and history, and common imaginings" (Kramsch 2014, p. 31). Earlier studies have also looked at the interplay between culture and language education (Lado, 1957, Kramsch, 1993) and the sociopolitical underpinnings of language use and practice as seen from national language preferences discussed in previous chapters. While there is the danger in oversimplifying the role of language in educational attainment over the more complex and contextualized factors that affect cognition and pedagogy, the inherent effect of this is recognized. For instance, Pierre Bourdieu and Jean-Claude Passeron's cultural capital and social reproduction highlight intrinsic advantages that can perpetuate societal structures from socioeconomic backgrounds that would enable better access to educational institutions, which can then further reinforce cultural factors (e.g., the "right" language).

Inseparably linked to power, opportunities, and control, the choice of a language defines broad consensus on access, from job prospect mobilities to better potentials in training and admittance to selective education institutions and greater political control in situations, among others. Thus, it is crucial to investigate the role of languages as it affects basic social services, interrogated in this book through the education sector. The vital weight given to language extends beyond this service sector approach. Still, it is also highlighted in broader political consensus, for example, as discussed through a "standardized" language in the ASEAN. Spanning from individual country cases where the language is deemed crucial for national unity, the perceived neutral position of English in the ASEAN bloc (Okudaira, 1999) ironically dictates its increasing global political influence. In the Philippines, contentions on language-in-education policies illustrate its authority and control. Notwithstanding the declared policy to use the national language (Filipino) more in government, business, and educational communications, divergence from its actual practice and use is documented (Friginal, 2007; Dumanig, David, and Symaco, 2012).

On the one hand, we see arguments on the need to uphold the English language for global competitiveness. At the same time, on the other, there is the desire to preserve indigenous languages through the multilingual approach in education. Both opposing views all but assert the impact of language in societal dynamics. This issue is illustrated in most (but not limited to) multi-ethnic countries where the choice of a national or official language follows the language of those in power (Dorian, 1998). In the Philippines' case, the choice of the national language as Filipino is linked with Manila, the country's center of political power. This elite closure in language strategy was defined two decades ago by Myers-Scotton (1993), identifying this social mobilization strategy when the "elite successfully employ language policies and their nonformalized language usage patterns to limit access of nonelite groups to political position and socioeconomic advancement" (p. 149)

Incidentally, the use of English within countries often linked to the elite and elite domains (Berg, Hult and King, 2001) also shows the increasing efforts of governments to train its population in the language to harness development advantages further deemed crucial. The continued globalization of services and the desire for standardization have emphasized the need to acquire the language of modernity (i.e., English), utilizing this to better compete in a knowledge society. And while the notion of multilingualism has gained traction in the past years linking this to better educational achievement (UNESCO Institute for Lifelong Learning, 2010), the oversimplification of attributing failure in education through language is all too often observed. The dismal performance of the Philippines in 2018–2019 international assessments illustrated this when the Secretary of Education herself announced the need to review the MTB-MLE policy in line with the requirement to improve the country's assessment scores. She also noted that Metro Manila and other provinces that use "English early" have performed much better in international assessments.

> It's an ongoing debate. Others want to continue the 'mother tongue' policy, while there are also those who say that we should start with English since English is the language of the rest of the world. So we are looking into this. (as cited in Galvez, 2019)

Such assertions also mirror the sociocultural implications of language, where the "center" can access better services and training compared to "peripheral" parts of the country, connecting this further to the cultural capital as espoused above. And while such results (i.e., dismal international performance) might run counter to the arguments raised earlier, where the Filipinos can secure better jobs and other opportunities due to their supposed language advantage, the discussion on the need to find the optimal language-in-education policy is evident. Despite this, the continuation of the MTB-MLE policy in tune for better teaching and learning and access to indigenous peoples (IP) of the Philippines continues to be pushed. Notwithstanding claims on the lack of training and resources required for a successful program (Monje et al., 2019), the Department of Education is "open to more dialogue for its improvement." And while this "waiting on the improvement" is noted, it has already produced education resources for 19 languages, which covers almost 80 percent of the learners' population. It is further set to develop more resources for IP languages. It is hoped that by the year 2027, "all of the estimated 180 IP languages will have their learning resources for MTB-MLE" (Department of Education, 2020). The push and pull of language-in-education policies in the Philippines require serious consideration of the situational realities of the country. Given its multilinguistic and desired socioeconomic objectives, such policy formations or reorientations must reflect and address such concerns.

CLOSING REMARKS

We have examined the various issues surrounding the role of education and language in the Philippines, from the view of development and modernization perspectives as heightened by increasing globalization to sociocultural and political dynamics alongside identity concerns. While it is tempting to offer solutions in education language policy with inclusion and access in mind, or for better education (e.g., through the MTE-MLB), the pressure compounded from the need to be globally competitive and to increase greater chances of mobility (i.e., English language proficiency) is also undeniable. The role of language as applied in social services such as education is made more complex with positions laying claim to poverty reduction at the same time. Studies that have looked at the role of language and poverty though rare are not new from Frederick William's 1967 collection of perspectives of the said theme to more recent explorations highlighting its relationship (Harbert et al., 2008; Perkins, Finegood, and Swain, 2013). Nonetheless, such an issue asserts equally essential concerns in terms of broader language policy. While fundamental human rights are linked to the utilization of multilinguistic features of a country, through the provision of better access and opportunities to services (again, through language use) that might otherwise be lacking in the dominion of a 'preferred' language, it is crucial to consider the lack of resources of poorer nations in its ability to optimize such a feature.

> how countries that are rich in ecological, cultural, and linguistic diversity but are economically poor can, with their limited financial means, satisfy both the human rights of their populations to evolve out of poverty and the alleged rights of their languages to each is used in the education system and/or other cultural domains. (Mufwene 2010, p. 914)

In the Philippines, despite the push for the MTB-MLE, critics time and again question the value of introducing such a policy because of the greater needs of the education system. On top of the broader and the introduction of the K to 12 education reform, this language-in-education policy competes in an already cash-strapped resource system (Symaco, 2013a; Reyes, 2010), additionally made vulnerable to disaster mitigation efforts where essential health and social services continue to lack. This view spans beyond just the Philippine setting when "economists have been reminding us of the enormous economic costs involved in dispensing education to every child in his/her mother tongue and the inability of developing nations' governments to assume the relevant costs" (Mufwene 2010, 923). When does the right to a language (i.e., mother tongue, IP languages, among others.) supersede the necessity for economic survival when its very essence requires the ability to master a language for global communications? And with matters concerning better education, how does one implement a rights-based approach over a country's need to rationalize its limited resources for other social services also deemed crucial? Despite intentions to find ways for children to better learn in schools through novel language-in-education policies introduced, we advocate the need to consider better situational actualities that exist. Only when we can balance the practical demands and resource abilities of countries like the Philippines in such context are we able to highlight 'ideological' requirements we regard lacking equally.

References

Abastillas, G. (2015). *Divergence in Cebuano and English code-switching practices in Cebuano speech communities in the Central Philippines*. [Master's thesis, Georgetown University]. Graduate School of Arts and Sciences, https://repository.library.georgetown.edu/bitstream/handle/10822/760907/Abastillas_georgetown_0076M_12963.pdf;sequence=1

ADB (2020). *Poverty data*: Philippines. Available at: https://www.adb.org/countries/philippines/poverty#:~:text=In%20the%20Philippines%2C%2016.6%25%20of,day%20in%202019%20is%202.7%25. (Accessed 28 June 2020).

Albano, E. (2020). Cordillera advocacy group urges rejection of Mother Tongue policy. *The Manila Times,* December 3, 2020. Retrieved from https://www.manilatimes.net/2020/12/03/campus-press/cordillera-advocacy-group-urges-rejection-of-mother-tongue-policy/804196/

Alberto, R., Gabinete, S., and Rañola, V. (2016). *Issues and Challenges in Teaching Mother Tongue-Based Multilingual Education in Grades II and III*: The Philippine Experience (April 22, 2016). Available at SSRN: https://ssrn.com/abstract=2768558 or http://dx.doi.org/10.2139/ssrn.2768558

Alidou, H. (2003). Medium of Instruction in Post-Colonial Africa. In James W. Tollefson and Amy Tsui (eds), *Medium of Instruction Policies: Which Agenda? Whose Agenda?* pp 195–214. Mahwah and London: Lawrence Erlbaum Publishers.

Alidou, H. and Brock-Utne, B. (2006). Experience I—Teaching practices –Teaching in a familiar language. In Alidou, H., Boly, A. Brock-Utne, B., Diallo, S.Y., Heugh, K., and Wolff, H.E., *Optimizing learning and education in Africa—The language factor*, pp. 854100. Association for the Development of Education in Africa (ADEA), http://unesdoc.unesco.org/images/0014/001460/146090e.pdf.

Alptekin, C. (1993). Target language culture in EFL materials, *ELT Journal, 47*(2), pp 136–143.

Alzona, E. (1932). *History of Education in the Philippines, 1565-1930*. Manila: University of the Philippines Press.

Ammon, U. (2001). *The Dominance of English as a Language of Science: Effects on Other Languages and Language Communities*. Berlin: Walter de Gruyter & Co.

Amin, A. and Thrift, N. (1995). Globalisation and institutional thickness. In P. Healey, S. Cameron, G. Davaoudi, C. Graham, and A. Madani-Pour (Eds.),

Managing Cities: The New Urban Context, Chichester, NY: John Wiley and Sons, pp. 91–108.

ASEAN Secretariat (2015). *ASEAN Economic Blueprint 2025*. Jakarta: ASEAN Secretriat.

Aspillera, P. (1981). *Basic Tagalog*. Manila: M. and Licudine Ent.

Axel, J. (2011). *Language in Filipino America*. Doctoral Thesis, Arizona State University, US. Retrieved from https://repository.asu.edu/attachments/56464/content/Axel_asu_0010E_10444.pdf

Azmi. I.A.G., Hashim. R., and Yusoff, Y.M. (2018). The employability skills of Malaysian university student. *International Journal of Modern Trends in Social Sciences, 1*(3), pp.1–14.

Baez, B. (2002). Learning to forget: reflections on identity and language. *Journal of Latinos and Education*, 1 (2): 123–132.

Baker, C. (1992). *Attitudes and Language*, Clevedon: Multilingual Matters.

Ball, S. (2012). *Politics and Policy Making in Education: Explorations in Sociology*. Abingdon: Routledge.

Bang, K.K. (2015). Inclusion in and through education: Language counts. *Jakarta Post,* February 21, 2015. Date Accessed May 25, 2021. https://www.thejakartapost.com/news/2015/02/21/inclusion-and-through-education-language-counts.html.

Bangko Sentral ng Pilipinas (BSP) (2015). *Economics and Financial Statistics*. Available at: http://www.bsp.gov.ph/statistics/efs_ext3.asp [accessed 8 November 2015].

Bangko Sentral ng Pilipinas (BSP) (n.d.). *Personal Remittances Grow by 2.5 Percent in October 2020; Cumulative Contraction Narrows to 1 Percent from 1.4 Percent in September*. Available at: https://www.bsp.gov.ph/SitePages/MediaAndResearch/MediaDisp.aspx?ItemId=5635 (Accessed 11 March 2021).

Bauman, Z. (2000). *Liquid Modernity*. Cambridge: Polity Press.

Baumgartner, J (1999). The controversy about the national language: some observations. *Philippine Quarterly of Culture and Society, 17*(2), pp. 168–172.

Bautista, M.L.S. (2001). *Defining standard Philippine English: Its status and grammatical features*. Manila: De La Salle University Press.

Bautista, M.L.S., and Butler, S. (2000). *Anvil–Macquarie dictionary of Philippine English for high school*. Pasig City: Anvil.

Bautista, M.L., and Gonzalez, A. (1986). *Language surveys in the Philippines: 1966-1984*. Manila: De La Salle University Press.

Bawa, L. (2020). The Effect of Job Enabling English Proficiency Administration on Philippine Students' English Language Skills. *International Journal of Education & Literacy Studies* 8 (1); 127–134.

Belvis, C., Morauda-Gutierrez, and Tzu-Bin Lin, M.R. (2019) Amorphous language as alternative model for multilingual education in the Philippines, *Cogent Education*, 6:1, DOI: 10.1080/2331186X.2019.1695998.

Benson, C. (2000). The primary bilingual education experiment in Mozambique, 1993 to 1997. *International Journal of Bilingual Education and Bilingualism*, 3(3), 149–166.

Benson, C. (2004). The importance of mother tongue-based schooling for educational quality. *Background paper for EFA Global Monitoring report 2005*. Paris: UNESCO.

Berg, C., Hult, F., and King, K. (2001). Shaping the climate for language shift? English in Sweden's elite domains. *World Englishes, 20*(3), pp. 305–319. DOI: https://doi.org/10.1111/1467-971X.00217

Bernabe, F.E.J. (1987). *Language policy Formulation: Programming, Implementation and Evaluation in Philippine Education*. Manila: Linguistic Society of the Philippines.

Bernardo, A.B.I. (2004). McKinley's questionable bequest: Over 100 years of English in Philippine education. *World Englishes*, 23 (pp. 17–31).

Bernardo, A.B. (2004). McKinley's questionable bequest: Over 100 years of English in Philippine education. *World Englishes, 23*(1), 17–31. doi: 10.1111/j.1467-971X.2004.00332.x

Bernstein B. (1962). Social Class, Linguistic Codes and Grammatical Elements. *Language and Speech*. 5(4), pp. 221–240. doi:10.1177/002383096200500405

Bernstein, B. (1971). *Class Codes and Control (Theoretical Studies towards a Sociology of Language, Vol 1)*. London: Routledge & Kegan Paul Ltd.

Bialystok, E. (2016). The signal and the noise: finding the pattern in human behavior. *Linguist. Approach. Bilingual.* 6, 517–534. doi: 10.1075/lab.15040.bia.

Bilingual education for young children: review of the effects and consequences. *International Journal of Bilingual Education and Bilingualism*. Pp. 1-14. http://dx.doi.org/10.1080/13670050.2016.1203859

Blaug, M. (1976). The Empirical Status of Human Capital Theory: A Slightly Jaundiced Survey. *Journal of Economic Literature, 14*(3), pp. 827–855.

Blommaert, J. (2006). Language policy and national identity. In T. Ricento (Ed). *An Introduction to Language Policy: Theory and Method*. Oxford: Blackwell Publishing, pp. 238–254.

Blommaert, J. (2005). *Discourse: A Critical Introduction*. Cambridge: Cambridge University Press. http://dx.doi.org/10.1017/CBO9780511610295

Bolton, K. and Butler, S. (2004). Dictionaries and the stratification of vocabulary: Towards new lexicography for Philippine English. *World Englishes*, 23 (1): 91–112.

Bourdieu, P. (1991). *Language and Symbolic Power*. Cambridge, MA: Harvard University Press.

Bowles, S. and Gintis, H. (1975). The problem with human capital theory: aAMarxian critique. *American Economic Review, 65*(2), pp. 74–82.

Brock-Utne, B. (2014). Language of Instruction in Africa: The Most Important and Least Appreciated Issue. *International Journal of Educational Development in Africa* 1 (1):4–18. https://doi.org/10.25159/2312-3540/2.

Brock-Utne, B. (2000). *Whose Education for All? The Recolonisation of the African Mind*. New York: Falmer Press.

Brock-Utne, B., and Hopson, R.K. (Eds.). (2005). *Languages of instruction for African emancipation: A focus on postcolonial contexts and considerations*. Cape Town, South Africa: Centre for Advanced Studies of African Society (CASAS).

Brohman, J. (1995). Universalism, eurocentrism, and ideological bias in development studies: from modernization to neoliberalism. *Third World Quarterly, 16*(1), pp. 121–141.

Burton, L. (2013). *Mother Tongue-Based Multilingual Education in the Philippines: Studying a Top-Down Policy from the Bottom Up.* Unpublished PhD dissertation. University of Minnesota. Available at: http://hdl.handle.net/11299/152603 (accessed 11 September 2020).

Butcholtz M. and Hall, K. (2004). Language and Identity. In A Duranti (Ed). *A Comparison of Linguistic Anthropology*. Oxford: Blackwell Publishing, pp. 369–394.

Byung-Jin, L. (2003). Education and National Identity. *Policy Futures in Education* 1(2), pp. 332–341.

Cabilao-Valencia, M.I. (2015). Filipino Marriage Migration. *SOSIOHUMANIKA: Jurnal Pendidikan Sains Sosial dan Kemanusiaan*, 8 (2), 161–170.

Cahill, M. (1999). From Endangered to Less Endangered: Case Histories from Brazil and Papua New Guinea. *SILEWP 1999-006*. [Online: http://www.sil.org/silewp/1999/006]

Calata, A. (2002). The Role of Education in Americanizing Filipinos. In H. McFerson (Ed.) *Mixed Blessing: The impact of the American colonial experience on politics and society in the Philippines*. Connecticut/London: Greenwood Press, pp.89–98.

Calvelo, G. (2020). *DepEd vows to address Filipinos' declining English proficiency.* ABS-CBN News. Date Accessed, May 25, 2021. https://news.abs-cbn.com/news/11/27/20/deped-commits-to-address-filipinos-declining-english-proficiency

Calzado, R. (2007). *Labour Migration and Development Goals: The Philippine Experience.* Workshop on "Making Global Labour Mobility A Catalyst for Development" Session II: Key Policy Elements in Comprehensive Labour Migration Management October 08, 2007, WMO Conference Center, Geneva.

Campesino, E. and Telen, J. (2014). A Geo-Linguistic Approach to a Historical Analysis of the Economic Trade-Partners of The Residents in the Zamboanga Del Norte and Misamis Occidental Strip. *South American Journal of Academic Research* 1(1): 1–7.

Casambre, N. (1982). The Impact of American Education in the Philippines. *Educational Perspectives 21* (4): 7–14.

Census (2010). *Languages in the Philippines.* https://www.ecensus.com.ph/. (2011.3.12).

Center for Migrant Advocacy (CMA), and Friedrich Ebert Stiftung Foundation (FES). (2009). *The Philippines: A Global Model on Labor Migration?* Retrieved from https://centerformigrantadvocacy.files.wordpress.com/2020/12/the-philippines-a-global-model-on-labor-migration.doc

CHED (n.d.). *ASEAN Indicators of Higher Education.* Available at: http://api.ched.ph/api/v1/download/2709 (Accessed 8 November 2016).

CHED (n.d. a). *Statistics.* Available at: https://ched.gov.ph/statistics/ [Accessed 30 January 2021].

CHED Memorandum Order 59 (1996). *New General Education Curriculum.* Pasig: CHED.

Chevalier, A. and Conlon, G. (2003) *Does it Pay to Attend a Prestigious University?* London: LSE.

Chimbutane, F. (2011). *Rethinking bilingual education in postcolonial contexts.* Tonawanda, NY: Multilingual Matters.

Chimbutane, F. and Benson, C. (2012). Expanded spaces for Mozambican languages in primary education: Where bottom-up meets top-down. *International Multilingual Research Journal*, 6(1), 8–21.

Chin, A. (2015). Impact of bilingual education on student achievement. *IZA World of Labor* 131. Pp. 1–10. Doi10.15185/izawol.131.

Civico, M. (2019). The Dynamics of Language Minorities: Evidence from an Agent-Based Model of Language Contact. *Journal of Artificial Societies and Social Simulation* 22(4) 3, 2019 Doi: 10.18564/jasss.4097 http://jasss.soc.surrey.ac.uk/22/4/3.html.

Chomsky, N. (2004). *Language and Politics* (edited by C.P. Otero). Edinburgh/Oakland CA: AK Press.

Christofis, N. (2019). World-Systems Theory. In: Romaniuk S., Thapa M., Marton P. (eds) *The Palgrave Encyclopedia of Global Security Studies.* Cham: Palgrave Macmillan. https://doi.org/10.1007/978-3-319-74336-3_372-1

Clemente, E. (n.d.). *Filipino Language in the Curriculum.* Available at: http://gwhs-stg02.i.gov.ph/~s2govnccaph/subcommissions/subcommission-on-cultural-disseminationscd/language-and-translation/filipino-language-in-the-curriculum/ (accessed 28 June 2020).

Clots-Figueras, I., and Masella, P. (2013), Education, language and identity. *Economic Journal,* Volume 123, Issue 570, pp. F332–F357.

Connor, W. (1993). Beyond Reason: The Nature of the Ethnonational Bond. *Ethnic and Racial Studies,* 16(3): 374–389.

Constantino, E.A. (1981). The Work of Linguists in the Development of the National Language of the Philippines. In Andrew Gonzalez and Maria Lourdes S. Bautista (eds.) *Aspects of Language Planning and Development in the Philippines.* Manila: Linguistic Society of the Philippines, pp. 28–39.

Crocco, O. and Bunwirat, N. (2014). English in ASEAN: Key effects. *International Journal of the Computer, the Internet and Management, 22(*2), pp.22–27.

Cruz, I. (2008). *Can we still count?* Retrieved from http://www.philstar.com/opinion/81960/can-we-stillcount.

Cullinane, M. (2020). *Philippines.* Available At: https://www.britannica.com/place/Philippine. (Accessed 28 June 2020).

Cummins, J. (2000). *Language, power and pedagogy: Bilingual children in the crossfire.* Clevedon, England: Multilingual Matters.

Cunanan, B.T. (2012), Voices from the Classrooms: Teacher Feedback on the Ubidization of the Philippine 2010 Secondary Education Curriculum. *Journal of English as an International Language,* 7 (2): 100–134.

Cunningsworth, A. (1995). *Choosing your coursebook.* Oxford: Heinemann.

Curran Daly & Associates (2019). *How 2020 Looks Like for the BPO and Shared Services Industry.* Available at: https://currandaly.com/2020-for-bpo-and-shared-services-industry/ (Accessed 11 December 2020).

Dastgoshadeh, A., and Jalilzadeh, K. (2011). Language loss, identity, and English as an international language. *European Journal of Social Sciences* 21(4):659–665.

Dayag, D. (2016). Preposition stranding and pied-piping in Philippine English: A corpus-based study. In G. Leitner, A. Hashim and H. Wolf (Eds), *Communicating with Asia: The future of English as a global language.* (pp. 102–119). Cambridge: Cambridge University Press.

Dayag, D. (2012). Philippine English. In E.L. Low and A. Hashim (Eds), *English in Southeast Asia: Features, policy and language in use* (pp. 91–100). Amsterdam: John Benjamins.

David, M.K, and Dumanig, F. (2008). Nativization of English in Malaysia and the Philippines. *Philippine Journal of Linguistics* 39: 67–79.

Dawe, C. (2014). Language Governmentality in the Philippine Education Policy. *Working papers in Educational Linguistics (WPEL)* 29(1): 61–77. https://repository.upenn.edu/cgi/viewcontent.cgi?article=1258&context=wpel

DECS order 52 (1987). *The 1987 Policy on Bilingual Education.* Manila: Department of Education, Culture and Sports.

Department of Budget (DBM) (2019). *2019 National Budget.* Available at: https://www.dbm.gov.ph/images/pdffiles/2019-People's-Budget-Quick-Glance_English-Version.pdf. Accessed 26 July 2020.

Department of Education (2020). *DepEd Open to More Dialogue on Improvement of MTB-MLE Implementation.* Available at: https://www.deped.gov.ph/2020/02/28/deped-open-to-more-dialogue-on-improvement-of-mtb-mle-implementation/ (accessed 28 June 2020).

Department of Education (2016). *Mother Tongue-based learning makes lessons more interactive and easier for students.* Retrieved from http://deped.gov.ph/press-releases/mother-tongue-based-learning-makes-lessons-more-interactive-and-easier-students.

DepEd (2015). *Department of Education Datasets.* Available at http://deped.gov.ph/datasets [accessed 8 November 2015].

DepEd (n.d.). *Historical Perspective of the Philippine Educational System.* Available at: http://www.deped.gov.ph/history (Accessed 8 November 2016).

DepEd (n.d. a). *Vision, Mission, Core Values and Mandate.* Available at: http://www.deped.gov.ph/mandate. (Accessed 8 November 2016).

DepEd Advisory 398 (2012) *Masters of Arts in Education Program with Specialisation in Mother Tongue-Based Multilingual Education.* Pasig: Department of Education

DepEd Order 16 (2012). *Guidelines on the Implementation of the Mother Tongue-BasedMultilingual Education* (MTB-MLE). Pasig: Department of Education.

DiMaggio, P. (1982).Cultural Capital and School Success: The Impact of Status Culture Participation on the Grades of U.S. High School Students. *American Sociological Review,* 47(2), pp.189–201

Djite, P. (2006). Shifts in Linguistic Identities in a Global World. *Language Problems & Language Planning* 30 (1): 1–20.

Dorian. N. (1998). Western language ideologies and small-language prospects. In L. Grenoble & L. Whaley (Eds.), *Endangered Languages: Language Loss and Community Response.* Cambridge: Cambridge University Press, pp. 3–21. doi:10.1017/CBO9781139166959.002

Dressler, C. and Kamil, M. (2008). First-and second-language literacy' in D. August and T. Shanahan (eds): *Developing Reading and Writing in Second-Language Learners: Lessons from the Report of the National Literacy Panel on Language-Minority Children and Youth.* Routledge

Dumanig, F. (2019). Bilingualism and multilingualism in primary education in the Philippines. In Lorraine P.S., Maria Teresa T., & Ian M. (Eds.). *Education and Childhood Studies.* Bloomsbury Publishing. DOI: 10.5040/9781474209472.0016.

Dumanig, F. (2015). Descriptive Analysis of the Surigaonon Language. *Polyglossia.* 27:1–10. doi:10.34382/00011430.

Dumanig, F. (2010). *Language choice in interracial marriages: The case of Filipino-Malaysian couples.* Dissertation.com: Boca Raton http://www.dissertation.com/book.php?method=ISBN&book=1599423677.

Dumanig, F. (2004). Phonological Differences of (f) and (v) Among Young Filipino Male and Female Students. *INTI College Journal,* 1 (4): 318–330.

Dumanig, F., David, M.K., and Manan, S.A. (2020). Transporting and Reconstructing Identities through Language Use in the Workplace: Focus on Filipinos in Malaysia. *Journal of Multilingual and Multicultural Development.* DOI: 10.1080/01434632.2020.1845707.

Dumanig, F., and David, M.K. (2014.) Miscommunication in Malaysian-Filipino Interactions: Intercultural Discourse in English. In Hajar Abdul Rahim & Shakila Abdul Manan (Eds.), *English in Malaysia: Post-Colonial and Beyond* (pp. 251–276). Frankfurt: Peter Lang.

Dumanig, F., David, M., and Symaco, L. P. (2012). Competing roles of the national language and English in Malaysia and the Philippines: Planning, policy and use. *Journal of International and Comparative Education,* 1(2), 104–115. doi: 10.14425/00.45.77.

Dumatog, R. and Dekker, D. (2003), *First language education in Lubuagan, Northern*Philippines, Manila: SIL International, available at:http://www.sil.org/asia/ldc/parallel_papers/dumatog_and_dekker.pdf

Durano, F. (2009). *Attitudes Towards English and Fil-English Code-Switching Amongst High School Student in Ormoc City, Philippines.* (Unpublished Master's Thesis). Malmö University.

Dutcher, N. (1995). The use of first and second languages in education. A review of international experience. *Pacific Island Discussion paper Series No. 1.* Washington, DC: World Bank.

Eberhard, D.M., Simons, G.F, and Fennig, C.D. (eds.). (2020). A language of the Philippines. *Ethnologue: Languages of the World.* Twenty-third edition. Dallas, Texas: SIL International. Online version: http://www.ethnologue.com.

Eder, J. (2004). Who Are the Cuyonon? Ethnic Identity in the Modern Philippines. *The Journal of Asian Studies,* 63 (3), pp. 625–647.

Edwards, J. (2009). *Language and identity: An introduction.* Cambridge, UK: Cambridge University Press.

Ellis, R. (1997). *Second Language Acquisition.* Oxford: Oxford University Press.

Eslit, E. (2017). Mother Tongue Based Multilingual Education Challenges: A Case Study. *Edelweiss Applied Science and Technology* 1 (1), 10–23.

England, K. (1996) "They think you're as stupid as your English is": constructing foreign domestic workers in Toronto. *Environment and Planning, 29*, 195–215. doi: 10.1068/a290195

Ertl, H. (2006) European Union policies in education and training: the Lisbon agenda as a turning point?, *Comparative Education, 42*(1), pp. 5–27, DOI: 10.1080/03050060500515652

Espada, J.P. (2012). The native language in teaching kindergarten mathematics. *Journal of International Education Research*, 8(4), 359–366.

Espada, J.T., Bayrante, J.R., Mocorro, R.E., Vinculado, O.P., Vivero, P.M., Bongcaras, L.L., and Labarrette, R.A. (2017). Challenges in the implementation of the mother tongue-based multilingual education program: A case study. *Research Journal of English Language and Literature*, 5(4), 510–527.

Espiritu, C. (2015). *Language Policy in the Philippines*. Available at: http://ncca.gov.ph/subcommissions/subcommission-on-cultural-disseminationscd/language-and-translation/ language-policies-in-the-philippines/ [accessed 8 November 2015].

Espiritu, C. (2007). *Language policies in the Philippines*. Retrieved January 1, 2020 from http://zzanggurl.blogspot.com/2007/06/language-policies-in-philippines.html.

Esteron, J.J. (2020). Language Attitude and Identity Construction of Trilingual Learners in a Rural School in the Philippines. *LLT Journal: A Journal on Language and Language Teaching*, 23 (1): 89 – 103.

Executive Order 134 (1937). *Proclaiming the National Language of the Philippines Based on the "Tagalog" Language.* Manila: Office of the President.

Executive Order 263 (1940). *Authorizing the Printing of the Dictionary and Grammar of the National Language, and Fixing the Day from Which Said Language Shall be Used and Taught in the Public and Private Schools of the Philippines.* Manila: Office of the President.

Executive Order 335 (1988). *Enjoining all Departments/Bureaus/Offices/Agencies/ Instrumentalities of the Government to Take Such Steps as are Necessary for the Purpose of Using Filipino Language in Official Transactions, Communications and Correspondence.* Manila: Office of the President.

Fairclough, N. (1989). *Language and Power.* Harlow, Essex: Addison Wesley Longman Limited

Fishman, J.A. (1972). *The Sociology of Language.* Rowley, MA: Newbury.

Glenn, C.L., and DeJong, E.J. (1996). *Language Minority Children in School: A Comparative Study of Twelve Nations.* NY: Garland.

Fishman, J. (1968). Nationality-nationalism and nation-nationism. In J. Fishman, C. Ferguson and J. Dasgupta (Eds). *Language Problems of Developing Nations.* New York & London: John Wiley & Sons, pp.39–51.

Fishman, J. (1977). *Advances in the Creation and Revision of Writing Systems.* The Hague and Paris: Mouton doi: 10.1515/9783110807097

Fishman, J. (1996). *What Do You Lose When You Lose Your Language?* Available at: https://files.eric.ed.gov/fulltext/ED395732.pdf [Accessed 22 November 2020].

Fitch, K. and Sanders, R. (2004). *Handbook of Language and Social Interaction*. New Jersey: Lawrence Erlbaum Associates.
Fletcher (1974). Evolutionary and developmental Sociology. In J. Rex (ed). *Approaches to Sociology: an introduction to major trends in British Sociology*. London: Routledge & Kegan Paul, pp. 39–69.
Freire, P. (1985). *The Politics of Education: Culture, power and liberation* (translated by Donaldo Macedo). Connecticut/ London: Bergin & Garvey.
Frignal, E. (2007). Outsourced call centers and English in the Philippines. *World Englishes, 26*(3), 331–345. doi: 10.1111/j.1467-971X.2007.00512.x
Gallego, M.K., and Zubiri, L.A. (2011). MTB-MLE in the Philippines: Perceptions, attitudes and outlook. *Frontiers of Language and Teaching*, 2, 405–414.
Galvez, D. (2019). *After Low PISA Result, DepEd Eyes English as Medium of Instruction in Primary Years (Inquirer)*. Available at: https://newsinfo.inquirer.net/1200113/deped-looking-into-english-as-medium-of-instruction-in-primary-years-after-low-pisa-result (Accessed 28 June 2020).
Gatil, T.B. (2021). Translanguaging in Multilingual English Language Teaching in the Philippines: A Systematic Literature Review. *International Journal of Linguistics, Literature and Translation (IJLLT)*, 4 (1), 52–57.
Geronimo, J. (2014). *No Filipino Subjects in College? 'Tanggol Wika' Opposes CHED Memo*, (Rappler) Available at: http://www.rappler.com/nation/110910-filipino-kolehiyo-repormakwf [accessed 8 November 2015].
Geronimo, J. (2015). *Pagtuturo at paggamit ng Filipino sa kolehiyo limitado pa rin (The Use and Teaching of Filipino in College is Still Limited)*, (Rappler) Available at: http://www.rappler. com/nation/110910-filipino-kolehiyo-reporma-kwf [accessed, 8 November 2015].
Geva, E. and Genesee, F. (2008). 'First-language oral proficiency and second-language literacy' in D. August and T. Shanahan (eds): *Developing Reading and Writing in SecondLanguage Learners: Lessons from the Report of the National Literacy Panel on Language-Minority Children and Youth*. Routledge.
Giles, H., Mulac, A., Bradac, J.J., and Johnson, P. (1987). Speech accommodation theory: The first decade and beyond. In M. McLaughlin (Ed.), *Communication yearbook* (Vol. 10, pp. 13–48). Beverly Hills, CA: Sage.
Gill, S.K. (2012) The Complexities of Re-reversal of Language-in-Education Policy in Malaysia. In: A. Kirkpatrick & R. Sussex (eds) *English as an International Language in Asia: Implications for Language Education*. Dordrecht: Springer, pp. 45–61.
Goffman, I. (2007). *Forms of Talk. Philadelphia*: University of Pennsylvania Press.
Goldsmith, A. (1995). The State, The Market and Economic Development: A Second Look at Adam Smith in Theory and Practice. *Development and Change, 26*, pp.633–650.
Goldthrope, J. (2007). Cultural capital: Some critical observations. *Sociologica, 2*, pp. 1–23.
Gonzales, W.D.W. (2017). Language contact in the Philippines: The history and ecology from a Chinese Filipino. *Language Ecology*, 1 (2), 185–212. DOI 10.1075/le.1.2.04gon

Gonzalez, A. (2003). *Language planning in multilingual countries: The case of the Philippines*. Paper presented at the Conference on Language Development, Language Revitalization, and Multilingual Education in Minority Communities in Asia. Retrieved from http://www.sil.org/asia/ldc/plenary_papers/andrew_gonzales.pdf.

Gonzalez, A. (1998). The language planning situation in the Philippines. Journal of Multilingual and Multicultural Development, 19: 487–525.

Gonzales, A. (1990). Evaluating bilingual education in the Philippines: Towards a multidimensional model of evaluation in language planning. In M.A.K. Halliday, J. Gibbons and H. Nicholas (Eds). *Learning, Keeping and Using Language*. Amesterdam/Philadelphia: John Benjamins Publishing Company, pp. 153–162.

Gonzalez, A. (1980). *Language and Nationalism*. Quezon City: Ateneo de Manila University Press.

Grace, G. (1989). Education: Commodity or public good?, *British Journal of Educational Studies, 37*(3), 207–221, DOI: 10.1080/00071005.1989.9973812

Graddol, D. (1997). *The Future of English?* London: The British Council.

Graff, H.W. (1969). *American imperialism and the Philippine insurrection (testimony of the times: Selections from Congressional hearings)*. New York, NY: Little, Brown and Company.

Grimes, B.F. (Ed.) (2000). 'Pakistan'. In *Ethnologue: Languages of the World (14th Edition)* Dallas, Texas: Summer Institute of Linguistics.

Grin, F. (1996). Economic approaches to language and language planning: an introduction, *International Journal of the Sociology of Language, (121)*, pp. 1–16. doi: https://doi.org/10.1515/ijsl.1996.121.1

Gumperz, J. (Ed.). (1982). *Language and social identity*. New York: Cambridge University Press.

Halliday MAK (1993). Language as Cultural Dynamic. *Cultural Dynamics*, 6(1-2), pp.1–9. doi:10.1177/092137409300600101

Harbert, W., McConnell-Ginet, S., Miller, A., and Whitman, J. (2008). *Language and Poverty*. Bristol: Multilingual Matters.

He, B. and Guo, Y. (2000). *Nationalism, National Identity and Democratization in China*. Aldershot: Ashgate.

Headland, T.N. (2003) "Thirty endangered languages in the Philippines," *Work Papers of the Summer Institute of Linguistics,* University of North Dakota Session: Vol. 47, Article 1. DOI: 10.31356/silwp.vol47.01

Herrera, D. (2015). The Philippines: An overview of the Colonial Era. *Education About Asia* 20 (1), 14–20.

Hoang, V.V. (2018) MOET's three pilot English language communicational curricula for schools in Vietnam: Rationale, design and implementation. *VNU Journal of Foreign Studies, 34*(2), pp. 1–25.

Hobsbawm, E. (1996). Language, culture and national identity. *Social Research, 63*(4), 1065–1080.

Holborow, M. (1999). *The Politics of English*. London: Sage

Hornberger, N.H. (2010). 'Language Shift and Language Revitalization.' In B. Kaplan (ed), *The Oxford Handbook of Applied Linguistics*, (2 ed.). Oxford: Oxford University Press, pp. 365–373. DOI:10.1093/oxfordhb/9780195384253.013.0028.

Hornberger, N. (1998). Language Policy, Language Education, Language Rights: Indigenous, Immigrant, and International Perspectives. *Language in Society, 27*(4), pp.439–458.

Hornberger, N. (1988a). *Bilingual Education and Language Maintenance: A Southern Peruvian Quechua Case*. Dordrecht: Foris Publications Holland.

Hintjens, H. (2008). Post-genocide identity politics in Rwanda. *Ethnicities, 8*(1), pp. 5–41.

Hu, R. (2016). The Age Factor in Second Language Learning. *Theory and Practice in Language Studies*, 6 (11): pp. 2164–2168, DOI: http://dx.doi.org/10.17507/tpls.0611.13

Huff, T. (2002). Malaysia's Multimedia Super Corridor and Its First Crisis of Confidence. *Asian Journal of Social Science, 30*(2), pp. 248–270.

Hurtado, S., and Carter, D. F. (1997). Effects of college transition and perceptions of the campus racial climate on Latino college students' sense of belonging. *Sociology of Education*, 70(4), 324–345. https://doi.org/10.2307/2673270.

Javier, J., and Vicerra, P. (2010). *Mashed media: Attitudes of secondary schools students towards English, Filipino, and their mother tongue*. Paper presented at 15th English in Southeast Asia Conference, University of Macau, Macau SAR China.

Jenkins, J. (2015). *Global Englishes: A Resource Book for Students*. New York: Routledge.

Jenkins, R. (2002) *Pierre Bourdieu* (2nd ed). London: Routledge.

Jernudd, B. (1999). *Language education policies—Asia. In B. Spolsky (Ed.). Concise encyclopedia of educational linguistics*. Amsterdam: Elsevier.

Johnson, A. (2009) The rise of English: The language of globalization in China and the European Union, *Macalester International, 22*(12). Available at: http://digitalcommons.macalester.edu/macintl/vol22/iss1/12 [accessed 8 November 2015].

Kang, H.-S. (2012). English-only instruction at Korean universities: Help or hindrance to higher learning? *English Today*, 109, 29–34.

Kaplan, R.B., and Baldauf, Jr. R.B. (2003). *Language and language in education planning in the Pacific Basin*. Dordrecht: Kluwer.

Kentjono, D. (1986). Indonesian Experiences in Language Development. In E. Annamalai, Bjorn H. Jernudd & Joan Rubin (eds.) *Language Planning: Proceedings of an Institute*. Mysore (India): Central Institute of Indian Languages.

Kirkpatrick, A. (2012). English in ASEAN: implications for regional multilingualism, *Journal of Multilingual and Multicultural Development, 33*(4), pp. 331–344, DOI: 10.1080/01434632.2012.661433

Kitsing, D. (2012). *Namibia's Language Policy is 'Poisoning' its Children*, (The Guardian). Available at: http://www.theguardian.com/education/2012/jan/10/namibia-english-crisis [accessed 8 November 2015].

Komisyon ng Wikang Filipino (KWF) (2015). *Mandato*. Available at: http://kwf.gov.ph/test/mandato/ [accessed 8 November 2015].

Komisyon ng Wikang Filipino KWF (n.d.). *Introduksiyon.* Available at:http://kwf.gov.ph/introduksiyon/ [Accessed 28 June 2020].

Koo, G.S. (2008). English language in the Philippine education: Themes and variations in policy, practice, pedagogy and research. Asia Pacific Journal of Research in Early Childhood Education, 2 (1): 19–33.

Kramsch, C. (1993). *Context and Culture in Language Teaching.* Oxford: Oxford Unversity Press.

Kramsch, C. (1998). *Language and Culture.* Oxford: Oxford University Press.

Kramsch, C. (2014). Language and culture. *AILA Review, 27*(1), pp. 3–55. DOI: https://doi.org/10.1075/aila.27.02kra

Krashen, S. (2003). *Explorations in Language Acquisition and Use: The Taipei Lectures.* Portsmouth, NH: Heinemann.

Kress, G. (1995). *Writing the Future.* Sheffield: National Association for the Teaching of English.

Kroskrity, P.V. (2000). Regimenting Languages. In P. V. Kroskrity (Ed.), *Regimes of Language: Ideologies, Polities, and Identities,* (pp. 1–34). Santa Fe, NM: School of American Research.

Kuo, M. M., and Lai, C. C. (2006). Linguistics across Cultures: The Impact of Culture on Second Language Learning. *Journal of Foreign Language Instruction,* 1 (1), 1–10.

Lacsamana, L.C. (1990). *Philippine History and Government* (Second ed.). Phoenix Publishing House, Inc.

Lado, R. (1957). *Linguistics across Cultures. Applied Linguistics for Language Teachers.* Ann Arbor MI: University of Michigan Press.

Lan, P.C. (2003). "They have more money but I speak better English!" Transnational encounters between Filipina domestics and Taiwanese employers. *Identities: Global Studies in Culture and Power, 10,* 133–161. doi: 10.1080/10702890304325

Lantolf, J (2000). *Sociocultural Theory and Second Language Learning.* Oxford: Oxford University Press.

Lareau, A., and Weininger, E.B. (2003). Cultural capital in educational research: A critical assessment. *Theory and Society 32,* pp. 567–606 DOI: https://doi.org/10.1023/B:RYSO.0000004951.04408.b0

Lartec, J.K., Belisario, A.M., Bendanillo, J. P., Binas-o, H. K., Bucang, N. O., and Cammagay, J.LW. (2014). Strategies and problems encountered by teachers in implementing mother tongue-based instruction in a multilingual classroom. *IAFOR Journal of Language Learning,* 1(1), 10–15.

Launio, R. (2015). Instructional medium and its effect on students' mathematics achievement. International Journal of Multidisciplinary and Current Research.3. pp. 462–465. Retrieved from http://ijmcr.com

Lawrence, L. (2020). The Discursive Construction of "Native" and "Non-Native" Speaker English Teacher Identities in Japan: A Linguistic Ethnographic Investigation. *International Journal of Society, Culture and language IJCL,* 8 (1):111–125.

Leaño, A.J., Rabi, N.M., and Piragasam, G.A.G. (2019). Speaking difficulties of Philippine indigenous learners in English Phonology. *International Journal Academic Research Business and Social Sciences*, 9(1), 1231–1244.

Levinson, S. (2003). *Space in Language and Cognition: Explorations in cognitive diversity*. Cambridge: Cambridge University Press.

Lewis, M.P., and Simons, G.F., eds. (2015). *Ethnologue: Languages of the World* (18 ed.). Dallas, Texas: SIL International.

Lewis, P., Simons, G., and Fennig, C. (Eds.). (2014). *Ethnologue: Languages of the World*. (17th ed.) Dallas, Texas: SIL International. Retrieved March 7, 2021, from http://www.ethnologue.com

Lewis, M.P., Simons, G.F., and Fennig, C.D. (Eds.) (2013). *Ethnologue: Languages of the World* (17th ed.). Dallas, TX: SIL International.

Liddicoat, A. (2014). Pragmatics and intercultural mediation in intercultural language learning. *Intercultural Pragmatics, 11*(2), pp. 257–277.

Llamzon, T.A. (1977). A requiem for Pilipino. In Sibayan, B.P. and Gonzalez, A.B. (eds.) *Essays in honor of Santiago A. Fonacier on his ninety second birthday*. Manila: Linguistic Society of the Philippines and Language Study Center of Philippine Normal College. 291–303.

Lobel, J.W. (2000). *An Introduction to the Languages of Romblon*. Unpublished Thesis.

Loheswar, R. (2019). *Reflecting on Failed MSC Plan, Kit Siang Urges Malaysia to Follow Bangalore's Lead*. Available at: https://malaysia.news.yahoo.com/reflecting-failed-msc-plan-kit-123317166.html (accessed 11 September 2020).

MacKenzie, P.J. (2009). Mother tongue first mutilingual education among the tribal communities in India. *International Journal of Bilingual Education and Bilingualism*, 12(4), 369–385.

MacMillan, D.W., and Chavis, D.M. (1986). Sense of community: A definition and theory. *Journal of Community Psychology*, 14(1), 6–23.

Madrunio M.R., Martin I.P., and Plata S.M. (2016) English Language Education in the Philippines: Policies, Problems, and Prospects. In: Kirkpatrick R. (Eds.) *English Language Education Policy in Asia. Language Policy*, (pp. 245–264). Springer, Cham. https://doi.org/10.1007/978-3-319-22464-0_11.

Magsambol, B. (2020). *Over 24 Million Filipino Students Back to School During Pandemic (Rappler)*. Available at: https://www.rappler.com/nation/filipino-students-back-to-school-during-coronavirus-pandemic-october-5-2020 (Accessed 11 December 2020).

Mahboob, A., and Cruz, P. (2013). English and mother-tongue-based multilingual education: Language attitudes in the Philippines. *Asian Journal of English Language Studies*, 1, 1–19.

Malone, D. and Malone, S. (2011). *Teacher Education for Mother Tongue1Based Education Programs*. Date Access January 2, 2021, at http://www.earlylearningtoolkit.org/sites/default/files/resourcefiles/Malone%20Teacher%20Ed.pdf

Marginson, S. and van der Wende, M. (2007). *Globalisation and Higher Education(OECD Education Working Papers, No. 8)*, Paris: OECD Publishing. DOI:10.1787/173831738240

Martin, I. (2020). Philippine English. In K. Bolton, W. Botha and A. Kirkpatrick (Eds). *The handbook of Asian Englishes* (pp. 479–500). New Jersey: John Wiley and Sons Inc.https://doi.org/10.1002/9781118791882.ch20.

Martin, W.M. and Lomperis, A.E. (2002). Determining the cost benefit, the return on investment, and the intangible impacts on language programs for development. *TESOL Quarterly, 36*(3), pp.399–429.

Martin, R. and Sunley, P. (1998). Slow Convergence? The New Endogenous Growth Theory and Regional Development. *Economic Geography, 74*(3), pp. 201–227.

Mateo, F. (2016). *Challenging Filipino Colonial Mentality with Philippine Art.* Master's Theses. University of San Francisco. https://repository.usfca.edu/cgi/viewcontent.cgi?article=1250&context=thes.

McCormick, P. (2019). Language policy in Myanmar. In A. Kirkpatrick & A. Liddocoat (Eds). *The Routledge International Handbook of Language Education Policy in Asia.* Abingdon: Routeldge, pp. 243–256.

McKenzie, R.M. (2010). *The Study of Language Attitudes.* New York: Springer Dordrecht Heidelberg London.

Menken, K. and Garcia, O. (2010). *Negotiating Language Education Policies: Educators as Policymakers.* London: Routledge.

Merriam, S. (1988). *Case study research in education: A qualitative approach.* San Francisco, CA: Jossey Bass.

Middleton, C. (2000) Models of state and market in the 'modernisation' of higher education, *British Journal of Sociology of Education, 21*(4), 537–554, DOI: 10.1080/713655369

Monje, J., Orbeta, A., Francisco-Abrigo, K., and Capones, E. (2019). *'Starting Where the Children Are': A Process Evaluation of the Mother Tongue-Based Multilingual Education Implementation.* Quezon City: Philippine Institute of Development Studies.

Mufwene, S. (2010). The role of mother-tongue schooling in eradicating poverty: A response to Language and poverty. *Language, 86*(4), pp. 910–932.

Mummendey, A., and Otten, S. (2001). Aversive Discrimination. In by R. Brown, and S. Gaertner (Eds.), *Blackwell Handbook on Social Psychology Vol. 4*, (pp. 112–132). Oxford, UK: Basil Blackwell.

Mustafa, Z. (2015). *The Tyranny of Language in Education.* Karachi: Oxford University Press.

Myers-Scotton, C. (1993). Elite closure as a powerful language strategy: the African case. *International Journal of the Sociology of Language, 103*, pp.149–163. DOI: https://doi.org/10.1515/ijsl.1993.103.149

Myles, J. (1999). From habitus to mouth: Language and class in Bourdieu's sociology of language. *Theory and Society, 28*(6), pp. 879–901.

Nakahara, K. (2006). The Socio-linguistics situation in the Philippines and the future of English and Filipino in the country. *Nature-people-society: Science and the humanities, Kanto Gakuin University* 40, 33–49.

Namanya, S.J. (2017). The effects of mother tongue-based multilingual education on the English literacy of children in Silang, Philippines. *International Forum, 20*(2), 160–177.

National Economic Development Authority (NEDA) (2017). *Philippine Development Plan 2017-2022*. Pasig City: NEDA.

National Statistics Office (2005). *Results from the 2000 Census of Population and Housing: Educational characteristics of the Filipinos.* Date Accessed January 4, 2021 at https://www.census.gov.ph/data/sectordata/sr05153tx.html

National Statistics Office (2002). *Results from the 2000 Census of Population and Housing: Educational characteristics of the Filipinos.* Date Accessed January 4, 2021 at https://www.census.gov.ph/data/sectordata/sr05153tx.html

Nebre, C. (2019). *Baybayin: Revival of Faded Characters.* Deped Division of Bataan. http://www.depedbataan.com/resources/4/baybayin_revival_of_faded_characters.pdf

Nical, I., Smolicz, J.J., and Secombe, M.J. (2003). Rural students and the Philippine bilingual education program on the island of Leyte. In J.W. Tollefson and A.B.M. Tsui (Eds.). *Medium of instruction policies: Which agenda? Whose agenda?.* Mahwah, NJ: Lawrence Erlbaum Associates.

Nolasco, R. (2012). *K+12 & MTB-MLE: Make haste, lay waste.* Philippine Daily Inquirer. http://opinion.inquirer.net/25095/make-haste-lay-waste. Accessed 5 November 2017.

Nolasco, R.M.D. (2013, September 13). "Castrated" MTB-MLE. *Philippine Daily Inquirer.*

Nolasco, R. (2012). *K+12 & MTB-MLE: Make haste, lay waste. Philippine Daily Inquirer.* http://opinion.inquirer.net/25095/make-haste-lay-waste. Accessed November 5 2017.

Nolasco, R. (2010), 'Filipino, Pilipino and Tagalog', in R Nolasco, F Datar, & A Azurin (eds), *Starting where the children are: a collection of essays on mother tongue-based multilingual education and language issues in the Philippines*, 170+ Talaytayan MLE Inc., Quezon City, pp. 170–172.

Nolasco, R. (2008). *The Prospects of Multilingual Education and Literacy in the Philippines.* Available at: http://www.seameo.org/_ld2008/doucments/Presentation_document/ NolascoTHE_PROSPECTS_OF_MULTILINGUAL_EDUCATION.pdf [accessed 8 November 2015].

Norton, B. (2009). Identity: Second language. In J. L. Mey (Ed.), *Concise encyclopedia of pragmatics* (pp. 358–364). Oxford, UK: Elsevier.

Obiols, M.S. (2000). *The Matched Guise Technique: A Critical Approximation to a Classic Test for Formal Measurement of Language Attitudes.* Date Accessed January 4, 2021 at http://www.cultura.gencat.net/llengcat.noves

Obondo, M.A. (2007) Tensions Between English and Mother Tongue Teaching in Post-Colonial Africa. In: Cummins J., Davison C. (eds) *International Handbook of English Language Teaching.* Springer International Handbooks of Education, vol 15. Springer, Boston, MA. https://doi.org/10.1007/978-0-387-46301-8_4.

Ocampo, D.S. (2017). *Mother Tongue-Based Multilingual Education (MTB-MLE) in the Philippines.* [Online] Available: from https://au.eventscloud.com/file_uploads/806b6ab12b0ebe095fa59e1d66b0cadf_Dina_ForARNECwthdinasrevisio ns02-03-2017finalfromkeynote.pdf June 19, 2018.

Okudaira, A. (1999) A study on international communication in regional organizations: The use of English as the "official" language of the Association of South East Asian Nations (ASEAN), *Asian Englishes, 2*(1), pp. 91–107, DOI: 10.1080/13488678.1999.10801020

Ordinario, C. (2019). *Communication Breakdown: Study Bares 'Weakness' in MTB-MLE Education System (Business Mirror)* Available at: https://businessmirror.com.ph/2019/07/04/communication-breakdown-study-bares-weakness-in-mtb-mle-education-system/ (Accessed 10 August 2020).

Oxford Online Dictionary (2019). Oxford University Press. Retrieved December 15, 2020.

Pang, E.F. and Hassan, R. (1976). Higher education and economic growth in Malaysia and Singapore. In A. Tapingkae (ed). *Higher Education and Economic Growth in South East Asia.* Singapore: Regional Institute of Higher Education and Development, pp. 3–56.

Papuc R.D. (2016). Language Variation, Language Attitudes and Linguistic Discrimination, *Essex Student Journal.* 8(1). doi: https://doi.org/10.5526/esj35

Parrenas, R. (2001) *Servants of Globalisation: Women, Migration, Domestic Work.* Stanford: Stanford University Press.

Parrocha, A. (2019). *Duterte signs Transnational Higher Education Act into law.* Available at: https://www.pna.gov.ph/articles/1081474 (Accessed 22 November 2020).

Paz, C. (1995). *Ang wikang Filipino: Atin ito.* Quezon City: University of the Philippines.

Penaranda, A.R. (2019). *Language as the Lifeline of Indigenous Identity and Transmission of Culture.* A side event organized by the International Presentation Association. April 23, 2019. Date Accessed January 4, 2021 at https://www.un.int/philippines/statements_speeches/%E2%80%9Clanguage-lifeline-indigenous-identity-and-transmission-culture-%E2%80%93-open-discourse

Pennycook, A. (2017). *The Cultural Politics of English as an International Language.* New York: Routledge.

Pennycook, A. (1998). *English and the Discourse of Colonialism.* London: Routledge.

Perkins, S.C., Finegood, E.D., and Swain, J.E. (2013). Poverty and language development: roles of parenting and stress. *Innovations in Clinical Neuroscience, 10*(4), pp. 10–19.

Perloff, R. (2003). *The Dynamics of Persuasion*, 2nd ed. London: Lawrence Erlbaum.

Phan, L.H., Kho, J., and Chng, B. (2013). Nation building, English as an international language, medium of instruction, and language debate: Malaysia and possible ways forward. *Journal of International and Comparative Education, 2*(2), pp. 58–71. doi: 10.14425/00.50.27.

Philippine Malolos Constitution 1899 (article 93).

Philippine (Republic of) Constitution 1935 (article XVIII, Section 3).

Philippine (Republic of) Constitution 1943 (article IX, Section 2)

Philippine (Republic of) Constitution 1973 (article XV, Sections 2 and 3).

Philippine (Republic of) Constitution 1987 (article XIV, Section 7).

Philippine Commission Act 74 (1901). *An Act Establishing a Department of Public Instruction in the Philippine Islands and Appropriating Forty Thousand Dollars for the Organization and Maintenance of a Normal and a Trade School in Manila, and Fifteen Thousand Dollars for the Organization and Maintenance of an Agricultural School in the Island of Negros for the Year Nineteen Hundred and One.*

Philippine Statistics Authority (PSA) (n.d). *Per Capita: Gross National Income, Gross Domestic Product and Household Final Consumption Expenditure.* Available at: https://psa.gov.ph/nap-press-release/sector3/Per%20Capita%20GNI (accessed December 3 2020).

Philippine Statistics Authority (PSA) (2021). *Updated Population Projections Based on the Results of 2015 POPCEN.* Available at: https://psa.gov.ph/content/updated-population-projections-based-results-2015-popcen (accessed May 21, 2021).

Philippine Overseas Employment Agency (POEA) (2015). *About POEA.* Available at: http://www.poea.gov.ph/about/aboutus.html [accessed 8 November 2015].

Philippine Overseas Employment Administration (POEA) (n.d.) *Philippines Overseas Employment Administration Deployed Overseas Filipino Workers by Country/Destination (total) 2015 vs 2016.* Available at: http://www.poea.gov.ph/ofwstat/compendium/2015-2016%20OES%202.pdf. (Accessed 28 June 2020).

Philippine Statistics Authority (PSA) (n.d). *Per Capita: Gross National Income, Gross Domestic Product and Household Final Consumption Expenditure.* Available at: https://psa.gov.ph/nap-press-release/sector3/Per%20Capita%20GNI (accessed 3 December 2020).

Phillipson, R. (1992). *Linguistic Imperialism.* Oxford: Oxford University Press.

Phillipson, R. (2015). Linguistic imperialism of and in the European Union. In H. Behr and Y. Stivachtis, (Eds) (2015). *Revisiting the European Union as an Empire.* London: Routledge, pp.134–163.

Psacharopoulos, G. (1988). Education and development: A review. *The World Bank Research Observer,* 3(1), pp.99–116.

Raco, M. (1998). Assessing 'institutional thickness' in the local context: A comparison of Cardiff and Sheffield. *Environment and Planning D: Society and Space, 30,* pp 975–996. DOI:10.1068/a300975

Rafael, R. and Rosario, F. (2011). *On language shift and revitalization: The case of Pangasinan.* Paper presented at the International Conference on Humanities, Penang, Malaysia.

Ramirez, J.D., Yuen, S.D., and Ramey, D.R. (1991). *Longitudinal study of structured English immersion strategy, early-exit and late-exit transitional bilingual education programs for language-minority children.* Final report to the U.S. Department of Education. San Mateo, CA: Aguirre International.

Ramos, T. (1979). *Studies in Filipino Second Language Acquisition.* Paper presented at the Summer Institute for Educational Research on Asian Americans (1st, Berkeley, CA, July 5-20, 1979).

Rappa, A. and Wee, HA (2006). *Language Policy and Modernity in Southeast Asia: Malaysia, the Philippines, Singapore and Thailand.* New York: Springer.

Rassool, N. (2007). *Global Issues in Language, Education and Development: Perspectives from Postcolonial Society.* Clevedon: Multilingual Matters.

Remittances (2021). *Migration data portal* (May 21, 2021), Date Accessed May 25, 2021 at https://migrationdataportal.org/themes/remittances.

Republic Act (RA) 8042 (1995) *Migrant Workers and Overseas Filipinos Act of 1995.* Republic of the Philippines.

Republic Act (RA) 9155 (2001). *An Act Instituting a Framework of Governance for Basic Education, Establishing Authority and Accountability, Renaming the Department of Education, Culture as Sports as Department of Education, and for Other Purposes.* Metro Manila: Republic of the Philippines.

Republic Act (RA) 10533 (2013). *An Act Enhancing the Philippine Basic Education System by Strengthening its Curriculum and Increasing the Number of Years for Basic Education, Appropriating Funds Therefor and for Other Purposes.* Metro Manila: Republic of the Philippines.

Reyes, A. (2017). Inventing Postcolonial Elites: Race, Language, Mix, Excess. *Journal of Linguistic Anthropology*, 27(2), pp. 210–231.

Reyes, V. (2010) The Philippine Department of Education: challenges of policy implementation amidst corruption, *Asia Pacific Journal of Education, 30*(4), pp. 381–400, DOI: 10.1080/02188791.2010.519696

Rivera, E.A. (2017). *Mother tongue-based mathematics Iloko language competence of grade 1 learners in Bauang district, division of La Union.* Paper presented at the International Conference on Education 2017. Doi: 10.17501/icedu.2017.3133.

Rivera, M.S. (2002). *The Matched Guise Technique: A Critical Approximation to a Classic Test for Formal Measurement of Language Attitudes.* Date Accessed January 4, 2021 at http://www.cultura.gencat.net/llengcat.noves

Rodriguez-Pose, A. (2013). Do institutions matter for regional development? *Regional Studies, 47,* pp. 1034–1047.

Rogayan, D.V. Jr. and Villanueva, E.E.N., (2019). Implementation status of K12 Social Studies program in Philippine Public Schools. *PEOPLE: International Journal of Social Sciences*, 5(3), 233–250.

Rosario, A., Gabinete, S., and Rañola, V. (2016). *Issues and Challenges in Teaching Mother Tongue-Based Multilingual Education in Grades II and III: The Philippine Experience* (April 22, 2016). Available at SSRN: https://ssrn.com/abstract=2768558 or http://dx.doi.org/10.2139/ssrn.2768558.

Rosekrans, K., Sherris, A., and Chatry-Komarek, M. (2012). Education reform for the expansion of mother-tongue education in Ghana. *International Review of Education, 58,* pp. 593–618. https://doi.org/10.1007/s11159-012-9312-6

Rost, M. (1994). *Introducing listening*. London: Penguin.

Rovira, L.C. (2008). The Relationship Between Language and Identity. The Use of the Home Language as a Human Right of the Immigrant Remhu - *Revista Interdisciplinar da Mobilidade Humana*, 16 (31): pp. 63–81.

Rubi, R. and Molina, M.C. (2020). Mother Tongue Based Multilingual Education: Implications on Teacher Readiness and Student Literacy. *Asia Pacific Journal of Education, Arts and Sciences,* 7 (4): 102–106.

Ryan, E.B., and Giles, H. (1982). *Attitudes towards Language Variations*. London: Edward Arnold.

Samuel, M. and Tee, M.Y. (2013). Malaysia: Ethnocracy and education. In L. P. Symaco (Ed). *Education in South East Asia*. London: Bloomsbury Academic, pp.137–155.

Samuelson, B.L. and Freedman, S.W. (2010). Language policy, multilingual education, and power in Rwanda. *Language Policy, 9,* pp.191–215 https://doi.org/10.1007/s10993-010-9170-7

Sapir. E. (1968) *Selected Writings of Edward Sapir in Language, Culture and Personality (D. Mandelbaum, Editor).* Berkley and Los Angeles: University of California Press.

Saville-Troike, M. (2003). *The ethnography of communication: an introduction. Volume 3 of Language in Society.* Oxford, U.K.: Blackwell Publishing.

Scherrer. C. (2005) GATS: long-term strategy for the commodification of education, *Review of International Political Economy, 12*(3), pp. 484–510, DOI: 10.1080/09692290500170957

Schluessel, E. (2010). History, identity, and mother-tongue education in Xinjiang. *Central Asian Survey* 28: pp. 383–402.

Schofer, E. and Meyer, J.W. (2005). The worldwide expansion of higher education in the twentieth century. *American Sociological Review, 70*(6), pp. 898–920. https://doi.org/10.1177/000312240507000602

Schultz, T. (1961). Investment in human capital. *The American Economic Review, 51*(1), pp. 1–17.

Seargeant, P. and Erling, E. (2013). Introduction. In E. Erling & P. Seargeant (Eds). *English and Development: Policy, Pedagogy and Globalization.* Bristol/New York/Ontario: Multilingual Matters, pp. 1–20.

Sellar, S. and Lingard, B. (2013). Looking east: Shanghai, PISA 2009 and the reconstitution of reference societies in the global education policy field. *Comparative Education, 49*(4), pp. 464–485, DOI: 10.1080/03050068.2013.770943

Sibayan, B. (1991). The intellectualization of Filipino. *Journal of the Sociology of Language*, 88, pp. 69–82.

Silverstein, M. (1998). Contemporary transformations of local linguistic communities. Annual Review of *Anthropology, 27*(1), pp. 401–426. DOI: https://doi.org/10.1146/annurev.anthro.27.1.401

Skutnabb-Kangas, T. (2001). The Globalisation of (Educational) Language rights. *International Review of Education 47,* pp. 201–219 https://doi.org/10.1023/A:1017989407027

Slaughter, S. and Rhoades, G. (2004). *Academic Capitalism and the New Economy: Markets, state and higher education.* Baltimore: John Hopkins University

Smits, J., Huisman, J., and Kruijff, K. (2008). *Home language and education in the developing world.* Background paper for EFA Global Monitoring 2009. Paris: UNESCO.

Solow, R. (1957). Technical change and the aggregate function. *Review of Economics and Statistics, 39*(3), pp. 312–320.

Smolicz, J.J. (1984). Is the monolingual nation-state out-of-date? A comparative study of language policies in Australia and the Philippines. *Comparative Education*, 20, 265–86.

Somblingo, R.A. andAlieto, E.O. (2019). English Language Attitude among Filipino Prospective Language Teachers: An Analysis through the Mentalist Theoretical Lens. *The Asian ESP Journal*. 24 – 41.

Spolsky, B. (2004). *Language Policy*. Cambridge: Cambridge University Press.

Spolsky, B. (2005). Language in its social context. *Journal of Baltic Studies, 36*(3), pp. 254–272.

Spolsky, B. (1999). Second Language Learning. In J. Fishman (ed) *Handbook of Language and Ethnic Identity*, pp. 181–192. Oxford: Oxford University Press.

Sta. Maria, F. (1999). On the teaching of English. *Journal of Asian English Studies* 2 (1&2): 84–89.

Stets, J., and Burke, P. (2000). Identity Theory and Social Identity Theory. *Social Psychology Quarterly* 63 (3): 224–237.

Stokes, B. (2017). *Language: The cornerstone of national identity*. Date Access, February 8, 2021. Retrieved from https://www.pewresearch.org/global/2017/02/01/language-the-cornerstone-of-national-identity/

Symaco, L.P. (2011). Philippines: Education for development? In C. Brock & L.P. Symaco (Eds) *Education in South East Asia*. Oxford: Symposium Books, pp. 139–155.

Symaco, L.P. (2012). Higher education in the Philippines and Malaysia:The learning region in the age of knowledge-based societies. *Journal of International and Comparative Education (JICE), 9*(1), p. 40–5. DOI: https://doi.org/10.14425/00.36.41.

Symaco,L.P.(2013).Geographiesofsocialexclusion:educationaccessinthePhilippines, *Comparative Education, 49*(3), pp.361–373, DOI: 10.1080/03050068.2013.803784

Symaco, L.P. (2013a). The Philippines: Education issues and challenges. In L.P Symaco (ed) *Education in South East Asia*. London: Bloomsbury Academic, pp. 191–212.

Symaco, L.P. (2017). Education, language policy and language use in the Philippines. *Language Problems and Language Planning, 41*(1), pp. 87–102. https://doi.org/10.1075/lplp.41.1.05sym

Symaco, L.P. and Tee, MY (2018). Social responsibility and engagement in higher education: Case of the ASEAN. *International Journal of Educational Development, 66*. pp. 184–192. https://doi.org/10.1016/j.ijedudev.2018.10.001

Symaco, L.P. and Tee, M.Y. (2019). Engaging forms of ASEAS higher education: Regionalism and governance. In D.S.L. Jarvis and K.H. Mok (Eds). *Transformation in higher education and governance in Asia*. Singapore: Springer, pp. 67–79.

Symaco L.P., and Wan C.D. (2017) Development of higher education in Malaysia: Issues and challenges. In: Samuel M., Tee M., Symaco L. (eds) *Education in Malaysia*. Springer, Singapore, pp. 53–66. https://doi.org/10.1007/978-981-10-4427-4_4

Tada, M. (2020). Language and imagined gesellschaft: Émile Durkheim's civil-linguistic nationalism and the consequences of universal human ideals. *Theory and Society 49*, pp. 597–630. https://doi.org/10.1007/s11186-020-09394-1

Tan, J. (2011). Singapore" school for the future? In C. Brock and L. P. Symaco (Eds) *Education in South East Asia*. Oxford: Symposium Books, pp. 157–175.

Tan, N. (2014). *What the PH Constitutions Say About the National Language*, Rappler. Available at: http://www.rappler.com/newsbreak/iq/65477-national-language-philippineconstitutions?cp_rap_source=ymlScrolly#cxrecs_s [accessed 8 November 2015]

Tecson, Z. (2020). *IP leaders, DepEd partner in educating youths amid Covid-19*. Department of Education. https://www.pna.gov.ph/articles/1119588

TESDA (n.d.). *Vision, Mission, Value and Quality Statement*. Available at: http://www.tesda.gov.ph/About/TESDA/11 (Accessed 8 November 2016).

Thomas, L., Singh, I., and J. Peccei. (2004). *Language, Society, and Power*. 2nd ed. London: Routledge.

Thomas, W.P., and Collier, V. P. (1997). *A national study of school effectiveness for language minority students' long-term academic achievement.* George Mason University, CREDE (Center for Research on Education, Diversity & Excellence). Retrieved January, 2021, from http://www.usc.edu/dept/education/CMMR/CollierThomasComplete.pdf

Thornborrow, J. (2004). Language and identity. In I. Singh and J. S. Peccei (Eds.), *Language, society, and power: An introduction* (pp. 157–172). New York: Routledge.

Tollefson, J. (1989). *Alien Winds: The Re-education of American's Indochinese Refugees*. New York: Praeger.

Tollefson, J. (1991). Language Planning and Language Inequality. New York: Longman.

Tollefson, J. (1993). Language policy and power: Yugoslavia, the Philippines, and Southeast Asian refugees in the United States, *International Journal of the Sociology of Languages, 103*, 73–95.

Tollefson, J. (2002). *Language Policies in Education: Critical Issues*. London: Routledge.

Torres, R.H.D. (2009). Effects of the Communicative Language Approach and the Use of Multi-media on Students' Grammatical Competence (Unpublished Master's Thesis). Notre Dame University, Cotabato City, Philippines

Trance, N.J., and Trance, L.A.M (2019). Embracing the K-12 Curriculum: Accounts of Philippine Teachers and Students. *Journal of Physics: Conference Series* 1254 012031: 1–9.

Triandafyllidou, A. (1998). National Identity and the Other. *Ethnic and Racial Studies*, 21 (4): 593–612.

Trudell, B. (2016). Local community perspectives and language of education in sub-Saharan African communities. *International Journal of Educational Development*, 27, 552–563.

Tsuda, Y. (2008). *English Hegemony and English Divide*. China Media Research, 4 (1), 47–55.

Tupas, T.R.F. (2003). History, language planners, and strategies of forgetting. *Language Problems & Language Planning, 27* (1), 1–25.

Tupas, T.R.F. (2008). Bourdieu, historical forgetting and the problem of English in the Philippines. *Philippine Studies*, 56 (1), 46–67.

Tupas, T.R.F. (2015). Inequalities in multilingualism: challenges to mother-tongue based multilingual education. *Language and Education, 29*(2), 112–124. doi: 10.1080/09500782.2014.977295.

Tupas, T.R.F. and Martin, I.P. (2016). Bilingual and mother-tongue-based multilingual education in the Philippines. In O. García et al. (eds.), *Bilingual and Multilingual Education, Encyclopedia of Language and Education*, DOI 10.1007/978-3-319-02324-3_18-1. Available from: https://www.researchgate.net/publication/307551787_Bilingual_and_Mother_Tongue-Based_Multilingual_Education_in_the_Philippines [accessed Jan 04 2021].

Tupas R., and Lorente B.P. (2014) A 'New' Politics of Language in the Philippines: Bilingual Education and the New Challenge of the Mother Tongues. In: Sercombe P., Tupas R. (eds) *Language, Education, and Nation-building*. Palgrave Studies in Minority Languages and Communities. Palgrave Macmillan, London. https://doi.org/10.1057/9781137455536_9

Turner, J.C. (1991). *Social Influence. Milton Keynes*, Open University Press.

Turner, J.C., and Oakes P.J. (1989). Self–Categorization Theory and Social Influence. In P. B. Paulus (Ed), *Psychology of Group Influence*, (pp. 233–275). New Jersey: Lawrence Erlbaum Associates.

Turner, J.C., and Onorato, R. S. (1999). Social Identity, Personality, and the Self–Concept: A Self–Categorization Perspective. In T. R. Tyler, R. M. Kramer, and O. P. John (eds). *The Psychology of the Social Self*, pp. 11–46. Mahwah, NJ: Lawrence Erlbaum Associates

Turner, J.C., Hogg, M.A., Oakes, P.J., and Wetherell, M., (1987). *Rediscovering the Social Group: A Self–Categorization Theory*. Oxford: Blackwell.

UNDP (2013). *Fast Facts: Indigenous Peoples in the Philippines*. Available at: https://www.ph.undp.org/content/philippines/en/home/library/democratic_governance/FastFacts-IPs.html (Accessed 28 June 2020).

UNDP (n.d.). *Goal 4: Quality Education.* Available at: https://www.undp.org/content/undp/en/home/sustainable-development-goals/goal-4-quality-education.html (Accessed 11 September 2020).

UNESCO (1953). *The Use of Vernacular Languages in Education.* Paris: UNESCO

UNESCO (2011). *Enhancing Learning of Children from Diverse Language Backgrounds.* Paris: UNESCO.

UNESCO (2018). *Aid to Education: A Return to Growth?.* Paris: UNESCO.

UNESCO Institute for Lifelong Learning (2010). *Why and How Africa Should Invest in African Languages and Multilingual Education.* Hamburg: UNESCO Institute of Lifelong Learning.

UNESCO Institute of Statistics (2020). *COVID19 A Global Crisis for Teaching and Learning.* Available at: https://teachertaskforce.org/knowledge-hub/covid-19-global-crisis-teaching-and-learning (accessed 28 June 2020).

UNICEF (1999). *UNICEF Annual report*. New York: UNICEF.

Valente, C. (2020). *Panelo Seeks Review of UP Technohub Deal*. Available at: https://www.manilatimes.net/2020/01/22/news/national/panelo-seeks-review-of-up-technohub-deal/676325/ (Accessed 15 July 2020).

Veltman, C. (1983). *Language Shift in the United States. Berlin*: Mouton.

Villegas-Torres, P. and Mora-Pablo, I. (2018). The Role of Language in the Identity Formation of Transnational EFL Teachers. *How,* 25 (2). https://doi.org/10.19183/how.25.2.418.

Vygotsky, L. (2012). *Thought and language.* Cambridge: MIT Press.

Wa-Mbaleka, S. (2014). English teachers' perceptions of the mother tongue-based education policy in the Philippines. *European Journal of Research and Reflection in Educational Sciences,* 2(4), 17–32.

Walter, S., and Dekker, D. (2011). Mother tongue instruction in Lubuagan: A case study from the Philippines. *International Review of Education,* 57(5-6), 667–683.

Watson, K. (2011). Education and language policies in south east Asian countries. In C. Brock and L. P. Symaco (Eds). *Education in South East Asia.* Oxford: Symposium Books, pp. 283–304.

Watson, K. (2012). South East Asia and comparative studies. *Journal of International and Comparative Education,* 1(1), pp. 31–39. DOI: 10.14425/00.36.42

Weedon, A. (2019). *The Philippines is fronting up to its Spanish heritage and for some it's paying off.* ABC News. August 9, 2019. Date Accessed, January 6, 2021 at https://www.abc.net.au/news/2019-08-10/inside-the-push-to-bring-back-spanish-into-the-philippines/11356590

Whitehead, D. (2013). *Lobbying for English in Indonesia Denies Children Mother-Tongue Education,* (the Guardian). Available at:http://www.theguardian.com/education/2013/feb/26/indonesia-mother-tongue-english-debate?INTCMP=SRCH [accessed 8 November 2015].

Williams, A.B, Metila, R.A, Pradilla, L.A.S. and Digo, M.M.B. (2014). *Strategies and challenges in MTBMLE implementation in the early years (Phase 1 Progress Report).* Quezon City: University of the Philippines and University of Melbourne

Wodak, R., De Cillia, R., Reisigl, M., and Liebhart, K. (1999). *The discursive construction of national identity.* Edinburgh, United Kingdom: Edinburgh University Press.

Woldemariam, H. and Lanza, E. (2014). Language contact, agency and power in the linguistic landscape of two regional capitals in Ethiopia. *International Journal of the Sociology of Languages,* 228, 79–103.

World Bank (2016). *World Bank Study Shows Shanghai's #1 Global Ranking in Reading, Math, & Science Rests on Strong Education System with Great Teachers.* Available at: https://www.worldbank.org/en/news/press-release/2016/05/16/world-bank-study-shows-shanghais-1-global-ranking-in-reading-math-science-rests-on-strong-education-system-with-great-teachers. [Accessed 1 August 2020].

World Population Review (n.d.). *Highest Catholic Population.* Available at: https://worldpopulationreview.com/country-rankings/highest-catholic-population (Accessed 28 June 2020).

World Risk Report (2018). *World Risk Report: Child Protection and Children's Rights.* Berlin: Bündnis Entwicklung Hilft/ & Ruhr University Bochum—Institute for International Law of Peace and Armed Conflict (IFHV).

Wrigley, H.S., Richer, E., Martinson, K., Kubo, H., and Strawn, J. (2003). *The Language of Opportunity: Expanding Employment Prospects for Adults with*

Limited English Skills. Available at: https://files.eric.ed.gov/fulltext/ED481481.pdf (accessed 10 August 2020).

Yadav, M.K. (2014). Role of Mother Tongue in Second Language Learning. *International Journal of Research, 11*: 572–582.

Young, C. (2002) First language first: Literacy education for the future in a multilingual Philippine society. *International Journal of Bilingual Education and Bilingualism*, 5 (4), 221–232.

Young, TJ., Sachdev I., and Seedhouse, P. (2009) Teaching and learning culture on English language programmes: a critical review of the recent empirical literature, *Innovation in Language Learning and Teaching, 3*(2), pp. 149–169, DOI: 10.1080/17501220802283178

Zainuddin, S., Pillai, S., Dumanig, F., and Philip, A. (2019). English language and graduate employability. Education + Training, https://doi.org/10.1108/ET-06-2017-0089.

Zohrabi, M., Sabouri, H., and Behroozian, R. (2012). An assessment of strengths and weaknesses of Iranian first-year high school English coursebook using evaluation checklist. *English Language and Literature Studies*, 2(2), 89–99.

Index

Addis Ababa Action Agenda, 19
access and inclusion, 65
access to education, 3, 5, 19, 27, 46, 66, 91, 94
acculturation, 25
actual classroom practice, 53, 56, 87
AEC Blueprint 2015, 21
Africa, 62, 74
Aguinaldo, Emilio, 3
Algeria, 24
alternative learning systems, 5
American, 3, 6, 37, 39, 45, 48, 87; colonial period, 3; colonial period, 3; occupation, 47, 87; Period, 46–47
Aquino, Corazon, 8, 66
Arabic, 24, 49
Association of South East Asian Nations (ASEAN), 8, 10, 21–23, 60–64, 90–92; ASEAN Economic Community (AEC), 21, 61, 90; ASEAN Qualifications Reference Framework (AQRF), 22, 90; ASEAN University Network (AUN), 21, 63; ASEAN+3 Working Plan, 22
Austronesian, 31–32
auxiliary languages, 7, 49, 51, 58, 75

Bahasa Melayu, 24, 34

Bangsamoro Autonomous Region in Muslim Mindanao (BARMM), 7
Baybayin, 45
Bengali, 24
bilingualism, 7; bilingual education, 7–8, 10–11, 29, 33, 35, 37, 39, 43, 51, 53–60, 63, 8169, 73; Bilingual Education Policy (BEP), 33, 37, 45, 47, 50, 54, 58, 75, 87; bilingual language policy, 6–7, 32, 64, 66; bilingual proficiency, 60
Bologna Process, 20
Bourdieu, Pierre, 11, 26–28, 69, 70, 76, 94
Business Process Outsourcing (BPO), 61
Brunei Darussalam, 60,

Cambodia, 22, 60, 61, 64–65
capital: cultural, 11, 26–28, 69, 94, 95; linguistic, 68–70
Cebuano language, 50, 74
China, 22, 63,
Christian nation, 1
cognitive development, 55
Commission on Higher Education (CHED), 4, 67
Commission on the Filipino Language, 7

commodification of education, 9, 11, 19, 66
commodification of educational services, 64
conditional cash transfer program (CCT), 19
contextualized language-in-education, 85
core-periphery approach, 17
corruption, 19
COVID-19, 83
culture, 3, 5, 7, 11–12, 16–17, 23–27, 43, 53–56, 64–68, 74–75, 86–90; cultural capital, 94, 11, 26, 27, 28, 69, 94, 95; cultural development, 25; cultural discontinuity, 29; cultural diversity, 73, 86; Cultural imperialism, 25, 62; cultural preservation, 24; cultural reproduction, 27, 28; cultural transmission, 30

Dakar Framework for Action, 18
democratization of education, 59
Department of Education, Culture and Sports (DECS), 4
developing nations, 18, 62, 96
development policies, 5, 21, 90
dialects, 24, 27, 46, 52, 73, 85
digital economy, 21
dominance of English, 32
Durkheim, Emile, 93

economic growth, 18, 43
Education for All (EFA), 16
endogenous growth theory, 20
English, 1; English as a Foreign Language (EFL), 26; English as a medium of instruction, 64; English as a working language, 61; English as the language for modernity, 28; English domination, 11; English language, 9, 10, 22, 28, 31–33, 36–38, 42–48, 52, 54–55, 59, 61–67, 69–71, 81, 88–93, 96; English language education, 36–38, 42–43, 89; English language training, 70; English proficiency, 33, 66, 87
enhanced basic education program, 58
ethnic diversity, 32, 61
ethnic languages, 31, 53, 60, 74–75, 77, 81, 86–88
ethnic origins of Filipinos, 74
European Union (EU), 63
European Higher Education Area, 21
exogenous approach, 20

Filipino, 1; Filipino accent, 42; Filipino ethnic group, 74; Filipino identity, 34, 39–44, 56–57, 75, 87–88; Filipino teachers, 46, 82
fluency of English, 91
foreign language learning, 25–26
formative years, 34, 43, 89
free public school system, 46
free-market, 90

General Agreement on Trade in Services (GATS), 90
globalization, 1, 8–12, 15–24, 33, 58–59, 63, 79; global competitiveness, 94; Global Englishes, 36

habitus, 26
hegemony, 11, 16, 61–62
higher education institutions (HEIs), 22, 66,
Hindi, 24
Human Capital, 9, 11, 17, 22, 27, 60, 69, 90; human capital development, 18–20; human capital theory, 16; human resources, 16, 21, 91; human resource development, 66; human resources training, 23
human rights, 96,

identity, 7, 11, 24–27, 31, 34–45, 51–58, 81, 85–89, 95–96; identity

construction, 35, 43, 81; identity formation, 8, 73; identity loss, 87
implementation of the MTB-MLE, 76
India, 24
indigenous languages, 32, 39, 70, 92, 94
Indigenous Peoples (IPs), 1
inequality, 11; language, 86; linguistic, 32; social, 63
information and communications technology (ICT), 59, 69, 91
Information Technology-Business Process Outsourcing (IT-BPO), 2
integrated ASEAN, 22, 63, 90
internationalization, 1, 10, 15, 16, 23–24, 59, 62
internet, 77, 79, 91
investment in education, 18

Japanese occupation, 4, 6

K to 12 (K12), 19, 37, 89, 96
Keynesian, 15
knowledge economy, 15, 21
Korean students, 61

language: attitude, 80; diversity in the Philippines, 76; endangerment, 24; loss, 24, 87; major languages, 48–49, 66, 73, 85; national language, 6, 10–11, 24–25, 27, 31–33, 36, 43, 46, 48–50, 53–54, 56, 58, 62, 64, 67, 70, 73–76, 81–83, 87–89, 92–94; neutral language, 33; minority languages, 50, 70, 76–77, 81, 86; of opportunities, 81; planning, 7, 86; plurality, 85, 86; policy, 6, 8, 10, 31, 33, 44–45, 47–49, 52–54,59–60, 63, 65–67, 69–70, 74–67, 82, 86–89, 93, 96; restoration, 24; transitional, 50
language education 26, 42, 57, 60, 71; English 31, 37, 42, 89; in the Philippines, 37, 86, 89; programs, 82; policy, 29, 44, 47, 85–86, 88 (*see also* language-in-education policies)
languages in the Philippines, 32, 47–48, 50–51, 58, 73–77, 79, 86
language-in-education policies, 8–12, 23, 45, 85, 93–97
Lao PDR, 61, 65
lingua franca, 75, 92
Lingua Franca Education Project (LFEP), 52
linguistic anthropology, 26
linguistic imperialism, 62, 87
Lubuagan First Language project/component, 7, 52
Luzon, 1, 31, 74, 85

Malay, 81
Manila, 1, 11–12, 22, 24, 50, 70, 94–95
Marginalization, 70
Marxist, 15
mass urbanization, 61
Marcos, Ferdinand, 6
McKinley, Wiliam, 10
migration, 74; labor, 43; skilled and unskilled, 52
Millennium Development Goals (MDGs), 18
minority language, 81; groups, 86; speakers, 51, 81
modernization theory, 16
mother tongue: education, 54, 78, 83; medium of instruction (MOI), 76; language, 55, 57, 76–77; languages, 44, 54, 58, 76–77, 79, 82–83, 88; materials, 83; teaching of, 55;
Mother Tongue-Based Multilingual Education (MTB-MLE), 6–8, 10, 12, 19, 29, 33, 37, 42, 43, 45, 47, 49, 52–59, 61, 64–66, 69–70, 73, 75–83, 88–89, 93, 95
multiculturalism, 25, 61
multilingual-based education, 23
Multilingualism, 49, 95
Multimedia Super Corridor (MSC), 21
Mutual Recognition Arrangements (MRA), 21–22, 63, 90
Myanmar, 61, 64

Namibia, 63
national identity, 8, 11, 31, 38–39, 42–44, 54, 88–89
neo-Marxist, 17
neoclassical economic frameworks, 17, 20
neoliberal, 19, 90
neoliberalism, 16
new comparative politics, 16
New Growth Theory, 9, 20

online education, 83
Overseas Filipino Workers (OFWs), 2, 67, 91

Pakistan, 24
Passeron, Jean-Claude, 94
Philippine bilingual language policy, 32 (*see also* bilingualism)
Philippine Constitution, 4, 6–7, 48–51, 54
Philippine English, 31, 37–44, 89 (*see also* Philippine Standard English)
Philippine languages, 31–32, 37, 39, 50, 74, 86
Philippine Normal College/School, 46, 48
Philippine Overseas Employment Administration (POEA), 68
Philippine Standard English, 37
Philippines Development Plan, 18
Pilipino, 6, 10–11, 48, 50
popularity of English, 87
post-modernism, 16
post-modernist approach, 9
poverty, 2, 4, 60
poverty reduction, 96
pre-colonial period, 45, 47
Programme for International Student Assessment (PISA), 19
public education system, 10

regional convergence, 20
regionalization of education, 20, 90
Romer, Paul, 20

rural areas, 92

salary differentials, 28
Schultz, Theodore, 16
Schurman Commission, 3
self-categorization, 35–36, 89; theory (SCT), 35, 58, 81
self-published books and textbooks, 79
Sinhala, 24
Smith, Adam, 17
social class, 26, 29, 42, 68
social identity, 25, 29, 35–36
social inequity, 27
social mobility, 29, 63
social reproduction, 93–94
Sociocultural approach, 24
socioeconomic advancement, 60
socioeconomic development, 15
sociolinguistics, 25
socioreligious conflict, 2
Southeast Asian Ministers of Education Organization (SEAMEO), 22
Spain, 3, 45, 47, 86
Spanish, 3, 6, 10, 32, 46–49, 57, 86–87
Spanish colonial period, 3
Spanish creole, 32
Spanish-American war, 47
speech community, 34–35
Sri Lanka, 24
Standard American English, 38
standardization of education, 85
Summer Institute of Linguistics (SIL), 25, 73
Sustainable Development Goals (SDG), 18

Taft Commission, 3
Taft, William Howard, 46–47
Tagalog, 6, 10–11, 24, 27, 31–32, 37, 39, 46, 48–50, 73–75, 85
Tagalog imperialism, 50
Taglish, 37–38
Tamil, 24
teacher training, 63, 65

Technical Education and Skills
  Development Authority
  (TESDA), 4–5
Thailand, 20, 61, 65
Thomasites, 3, 46–47
Timor-Leste, 61, 65
Transnational Higher Education Law,
  19, 21, 23, 66
Treaty of Paris, 47
Trends in International Mathematics and
  Science Study (TIMSS), 19

United Nations, 1, 63
United States of America (USA), 3, 16,
  45, 47, 62, 75

Universal Access to Quality Tertiary
  Education Act, 19
universal primary education, 18
university rankings system, 19
Urdu, 24

Vietnam, 61, 64–65
Visayas, 1, 31–32, 50, 74, 85
Vygotsky, Lev, 24

Wallerstein, Immanuel, 17
World Englishes, 36
World Trade Organisation (WTO), 1, 90

About the Authors

Lorraine Pe Symaco is ZJU 100 professor at Zhejiang University, China. Prior to this, she was she was founder-director of the Centre for Research in International and Comparative Education (CRICE) and UNESCO Chair in International and Comparative Educational Research with Special Reference to South East Asia at the University of Malaya, Malaysia.

Francisco Perlas Dumanig is an assistant professor of English and TESOL Coordinator at the University of Hawaii at Hilo, USA. He has done research on Language and Identity of Economic Migrants, English Language Teaching and Learning (ENL, ESL, and EFL), Language Planning and Language Policy, and Southeast Asian Englishes.

www.ingramcontent.com/pod-product-compliance
Lightning Source LLC
Chambersburg PA
CBHW020127010526
44115CB00008B/1016